REGENT PRESS

CONTACT: Mark Weiman

M000035265

FOR FAVOR OF REVIEW

TITLE: **A MAXIM MAP OF MANHATTAN**
AUTHOR: Kimo RedeR
PUB. DATE: January 1, 2023
ISBN-13:   paperback: 978-1-58790-638-1
             e-book: 978-1-58790-639-8 (forthcoming)
PAGES: 128 pages / paperback / 6" x 9"
COST: paperback $18.00 / e-book $9.95

ABOUT THE BOOK

A Maxim Map of Manhattan is a mosaic portrait of one of our planet's most iconic urban settings. Dense and teeming like the island borough it depicts, its pages form a collage of offbeat witticisms, concocted vignettes, and surreal social critiques grouped into thematic neighborhoods.

Spinning an alternative and non-linear history, this parody of a tourist guide serenades its target locale's renegade spirit and offers up an ode of praise to its noted talent for reinvention. The book's fragmentary format spans an eclectic range of topics, including public art, global dialects, seasonal wardrobe, macroeconomics, civil engineering, and culinary trends on its over spilling menu.

While Manhattan resists being truly captured by any single profile, several of its key features are productively distorted in this gallery of funhouse mirrors. *A Maxim Map of Manhattan* "maps" not by laying down grid lines of latitude and longitude, but by playfully assembling its pieces into a deliberately bottomless puzzle.

ABOUT THE AUTHOR

Kimo RedeR is a widely published scholar and poet/essayist and an Associate Professor of English at the City University of New York's Borough of Manhattan campus. His current writing projects include a series of esoteric meditations on the human hand, an inverted account of the Tower of Babel, and an index of post-Wittgensteinian "rogue linguistics."

A Maxim Map
of Manhattan

A Maxim Map
of Manhattan

Kimo RedeR

REGENT PRESS
Berkeley, California
2022

[paperback]
ISBN 13: 978-1-58790-638-1
ISBN 10: 1-58790-638-4

[e-book]
ISBN 13: 978-1-58790-639-8
ISBN 10: 1-58790-639-2

Library of Congress Control Number: 2022038697

Cover Artwork *New York City Street Map*
courtesy of Michael Tompsett

Back Cover Art: *Manhattan Map Origami Squirrel and Pigeon*
courtesy of Twink Reder

Manufactured in the U.S.A.
Regent Press
Berkeley, CA
www.regentpress.net

THIS BOOK IS DEDICATED
TO ALL OF MY NEW YORK CITY ANCESTORS

A Maxim Map of Manhattan's *early blueprints benefited greatly from the encouragements of my colleagues Andrew Levy, Cheryl J. Fish, Robert Lapides, Margaret Barrow, Stephen doCarmo, Benita Noveno, and the Flying Rubin Brothers, Alan and Richard.*

* * *

My wife Twink Reder contributed her invaluable editorial acuity and cartographic savvy to this work, and folded its origami mascots into being. Our walks along Manhattan's waterfronts inspired many of the aphorisms that were the seedlings for the book's eventual blossoming.

The "New" in ever-innovating New York City seems to take itself more literally than the "New" in New Hampshire does, but the "York" in New York City takes itself less literally than the "Orleans" does in Francophilic New Orleans.

Manhattan's geologic foundation is a triple-layer cake
        of Manhattan Schist, Inwood Marble, and Fordham Gneiss
used to celebrate the borough's epic survival, daily rebirths,
        and nano-second anniversaries .

If some Egyptian god's corpse were scattered across Manhattan,
    his wristbone would be buried under a MOMA mural
        and his ribs under a midtown steakhouse
            his navel at Columbus Circle
                and his eyes distributed as security cameras
            until the Hudson is prepared to flood like the Nile.

The elbows of a midtown pedestrian-crossing icon form an angle that is half Roaring Twenties Charleston and half grave digger paused in mid-dig. In Manhattan, dividing the pedestrians you pass on the street into potential role models and potential warning signs will leave an unsightly center crease in your own personality.

⅏ ⅏ ⅏ ⅏ ⅏ ⅏ ⅏ ⅏ ⅏ ⅏ ⅏ ⅏

From an animist perspective on Manhattan nomenclature
    "North of Madison"
        abbreviated as "NoMad"
            tempts Vesey, Gramercy, Bowery, and Delancey
                to contort into "V(a)G(a)B(on)D."

Once term limits disqualify New York as a candidate for Premiere City of the 22nd Century, it will feel free to nominate itself as a candidate for Metropole of the Millennium, Design House of the Holocene Epoch, and Pharaoh-Throne of the Phanerozoic Eon.

Perhaps Times Square hotel ear-plugs will come equipped with decibel-counters when Times Square hotel sleep-masks come with photon-refractors. In an Ian Fleming version of a mid-sized Times Square business firm, a CEO isn't granted a shoe-phone or a cane-sword or a cuticle-camera till he has earned his own dossier of international enemies.

In Times Square, the directions given to lost tourists
    seem to feature more hand gestures and less adjectives
        and more head-shakes and less map-consultations
            than the directions given to lost tourists in Central Park.

ᵇᵇᵇᵇᵇᵇᵇᵇᵇᵇᵇᵇᵇᵇᵇᵇᵇᵇᵇᵇᵇᵇᵇ

The occasional animal that escapes from a square cage in the Central Park Zoo is baffled and encouraged by the lack of rectitude in the respective geometries of Times, Herald, Washington, and Tompkins Squares.

In a Times Square horde, the "ill" in "standstill"
        and in "treadmill" tend to overlap
            because Times Square runs on kosher-deli dillowatts
                and dive-bar swillowatts
                    and charge-me-later billowatts
                        as well as Con-Edison kilowatts.

The X's that used to festoon 1970's
   Times Square movie marquees
      are an endangered species hoping for musical revivals
         of *The Little Foxes*, *Xanadu* and *Taxi Driver*
            to prolong their lifespan in the city's letterscape.

When Las Vegas replicates Manhattan monuments faster than New York can produce them, Times Square needs to go on triple overtime.

****

The plastic capes in Manhattan's barber shops are now red, gold, and green as often as they are red, white, and green, in a kind of oblique rejoinder to Italy's occupation of Ethiopia. If a Little Abyssinia ever manages to usurp Little Italy, Chinatown may consider waging a small-scale Boxer Rebellion against the Sony building.

Italian tourists who pose for photographs
   as if holding up the Leaning Tower of Pisa
      also insist on saluting a Jasper Johns flag at the Whitney
         and making spooning gestures
            toward a Warhol soup can at MoMA.

In an affront to New York's blueblood registries and home-town chauvinism, glacial erratics—non-native boulders deposited onto the landscape during the most recent Ice Age—may arguably be Manhattan Island's longest-lived immigrants. For more recent European immigrants, a transatlantic steamer's vertical smoke-stacks were skyscraper-previews writ small.

Mah-jongg played in Chinatown's Columbus Park
    is an Asian game
        named after sparrows
            and played in a pigeon-dominated plaza
                named for a non-discoverer
                    of the so-called Orient.

.:.:.:.:.:.:.:.:.:.:.:.:.:.:.:.

If Berlin's Brandenburg Gate and the triumphal Arch at Washington Square Park's north entrance switched places, the East Village and the Upper West Side would remain equally remote from one another but the concept of international monument exchange would make its greatest stride since London Bridge was transplanted to Arizona.

During an axe-murder investigation, "A" remains the most common letter formed by a police-barricade sawhorse and "X" the most common letter made out of crime-scene police tape and "E" the letter most closely resembling a two-story tenement sawn in half.

The bench-to-tree ratio in Central Park continues at approximately 1-to-3, the same ratio of vermouth to brandy in a Manhattan cocktail. The park's width is spanned by several east-to-west transverse roads that can be figuratively viewed as the Tropics of Caviar, Cacophony, College, and Cathedral.

Contract Manhattan to the size of a breadcrumb
    and Central Park becomes a large patch of penicillin mold:
        expand Manhattan to the size of the planet
    and Central Park becomes the Amazonian rainforest
        multiplied by sub-Saharan Africa.

The pedigree of the average upper Central Park poodle has so many post-scripts it has a hard time fitting onto its flea collar. At the Central Park zoo, non-captive animals like pigeons and squirrels exhibit some intriguingly in-between ambivalences about their imprisoned ancestors.

That August sun that can soften Columbus Circle asphalt
    back into tar
is not so retro-active it can uncut a Delmonico's sirloin
    back into an Aberdeen angus cow
or unlace a Central Park pretzel
    back into a stalk of durum wheat.

∧∧∧∧∧∧∧∧∧∧∧∧∧∧∧∧∧∧∧∧∧∧∧∧∧∧∧∧∧∧

I "Heart" New York tourist paraphernalia would more accurately be I "Liver Transplant" New York in proximity to Upper East Side watering holes and I "Heaving Lung" New York in proximity to Central Park's jogging trails.

Suitably, the man who was hired to survey Manhattan
    to prepare for its easy-grip grid system
    had a surname that rhymes with "handle,"
and the man who designed Central Park
    from the depths of his own visionary cranium
    had a surname that rhymes with "head."

The second "a" in "Haarlem" and the second "a" in "Mannahatta" migrated to the same vowel Valhalla when they died. New York City merges the "pell" in "pell mell" and the "pel" in "archipelago" because its collective neuroses are products of the "tic" in "vertical" and the "row" in "overcrowded."

In order to qualify as fully streetwise to Manhattan,
    one must be fleetwise towards its taxi-meters
        meatwise towards its artisanal butchers" scales
           and heatwise towards its grating-emissions.

□□□□□□□□□□□□□□□□□□□□□□□□□□□□□□□□□□□

In Manhattan, "waitstaff" curdles into "hatestaff" much more quickly than "valet parking" has a chance to ascend into "chalet parking." "Influence peddling" becomes "influence pedaling" on the wheels of fortune and finance and most of what is perceived by an elderly dog-walker as a "scare tactic" is merely a newly trending "flair tactic."

Two of the historically twinkling stars in Manhattan's entertainment constellation, the Cotton Club and the Pyramid Club, both referred back to shameful episodes of forced slave labor despite their otherwise-distracted dancefloors.

ΛΛΛΛΛΛΛΛΛΛΛΛΛΛΛΛΛΛΛΛΛΛΛΛΛΛΛΛ

Manhattan's various eyes in the sky can locate the whereabouts and whenabouts of pedestrians, but rarely ascertain their whyabouts or howabouts. Manhattan's eavesdropping equipment can amplify a sigh into a sonic boom but reduce a cry for assistance into an echo bounced off the Wall of Indifference.

Ralph Waldo Emerson referred to New York City as "a sucked orange" several decades before Big Apple bumper-stickers, coffee-mugs, and T-shirts, getting the general metaphor right but the precise fruit wrong, erring on the side of Citrus instead of Cider.

Can any single poll or study prove that the sign of the cross is made with a more pursed and staccato flourish of the hands in Spanish Harlem than in Morningside Heights? Would any chemical analysis reveal that city-jail visitor name tags sport a marginally more neurotoxic adhesive backing than trading-floor visitor name tags?

Does how many "allegedly"'s a white-collar buccaneer can juggle before his tax shelter suffers a roof collapse or a basement flood depend on how many "purported"'s a New York Post article can handle before its legal team starts dreaming in libel?

≈∞≈∞≈∞≈∞≈∞≈∞≈∞≈∞≈∞≈∞

What sort of blood-flow-to-traffic-flow conversion table could determine if Manhattan's streets are its veins and its avenues its arteries or vice versa? Is the vertical crease separating the odd pages from the even pages of the *New Yorker* the magazine's scale equivalent of 5th Avenue?

Can a savvy-enough Pearl St. jeweler's microscope see
    a debit column inside of a diamond or a retirement plan
        inside of a ruby?
    An earnings-allowance inside of an emerald
        or a sales draft inside of a sapphire?

<><><><><><><><><><><><><><>

Is every pause in a New York politician's prepared statement proof that perjury is always a pursed pair of lips away from picketing itself? Is every other use of "henceforth" in said statement proof that there are post-crastinations as well as procrastinations in said politico's arsenal?

If the incomplete dinosaur skeletons at the Museum of Natural History can be said to figuratively suffer from phantom ten-foot tibia sensation, can the fossil footprints of mastodons be seen as remote precursors of the post-Jurassic urban pothole?

The taller the skyscraper, the more its need for horizontal sway, and so theoretically a tower reaching to the moon would need to sway from the North Pole to the South Pole to prevent itself from cracking in two. The shadow that a skyscraper ideally "wants" to cast usually gets blocked and swallowed by its neighbors, making Manhattan an exercise in *umbrus interuptus*.

If Manhattan is indeed a "skyscraper soup"
(in William Carlos Williams" phrase),
    it is also more specifically a "granite gumbo,"
        a "building borscht,"
            and a "monetary minestrone."

«±«±«±«±«±«±±«±«±«±«±«±«±«±«±«±«

Advice to amateur surrealists: taking a photograph of the Manhattan skyline through the giant aquarium tanks in Staten Island's ferry lobby will give the illusion of giant eels and catfish swimming around the iconic skyscrapers far in the background.

New York's suicidal lover's-leaps grow progressively less tall
—from skyscrapers to cliff-sides to treetops to stepladders—
as cell phones add more and more comforting
and distracting features.

The cornerstones of skyscrapers have occasionally been known to evade questions about their historic age, like a scroll found in a Palestinian vase or a Park Avenue trophy widow. The mere mention of the word "skyscraper" can cause a carpenter's tape-measure to want to curl back into its casing.

If Manhattan's cabbies are regulated by "hack licenses,"
    its skyscraper-planners should be regulated by "stack licenses"
        and its suit-delivering garment workers by "rack licenses."

In one of midtown's signature traffic-jams,
Hesitation's hood ornament has a hard time
 keeping ahead of Remorse's rear fender
and Trepidation's turn-signal has a hard time communicating
with Belligerence's still-healing bumper.

Alongside its errand-runners, midtown Manhattan also features errand-chasers, and errand-hurdlers whose idea of a post-lunch siesta is a quick blink, a wet-comb, and a tie-straightening. Round off every corner of every midtown intersection and their sense of transition will be made gentler but their sense of navigation will grow blurrier.

ʃʃʃ

The morgues under midtown Manhattan contain fresh cadavers still capable of dreaming of a better spot in line at Elaine's or a better dividend on a particular mutual fund. Consequently, down-town-designer DNA will flood the mid-town mitochondria market before curbside custom-made chromosomes.

Large enough objects have a mass
able to warp the fabric of space/time,
and some public-plaza Manhattan sculptures have enough mass
to distend the fabric of a midtown lunch hour

The embossed letters on a midtown manhole cover can impress themselves on the summer-softened rubber of a truck-tire and travel out of town to spread the Manhattan gospel into the also-pliant suburbs, the half-receptive exurbs, and the asphalt-evading outback.

For every Not in Kansas Anymore,
    midtown Manhattan boasts a
        Not in Casablanca For Decades
           a Not Yet in Kathmandu
               and a Not On Your Life in Calcutta.

Sometimes Manhattan is a comedian's one-liner waiting for its words to self-assemble, sometimes it is a filibuster piling on semicolons to slow down its finale. Sometimes Manhattan is a Dantean dumpster-fire set on top of a discontinued dinosaur turnpike, sometimes it is a Cartesian lattice pulsating in accord with the old Indian footpaths.

Frequently the median paragraph of a ten-column Times editorial
    contains a surefire recipe for a pending Armageddon
        or a too-fast gesture toward a slow-motion cultural mutiny
           that goes underread, ill-noticed, and unacted on.

í⟩í⟩í⟩í⟩í⟩í⟩í⟩í⟩í⟩í⟩í

Sometimes Manhattan is a handicapped parking space willing to convert into a helipad at a half-moment's notice. Sometimes Manhattan is a suggestion box with its false bottom poised over a titanium-fanged paper-shredder.

Generally, rosaries are fingered with more emphasis
on the decisive index finger
    in the highrises along Morningside Heights
    and with more emphasis on the
        ruddering, steadying thumb
            in the brownstones of Spanish Harlem.

:.

Sometimes an urban hermit's grocery list grows so long its
eggs hatch before its milk curdles and its bread turns to penicillin before its penicillin goes impotent. Sometimes an upper-crust
Tribeca piñata comes packed from its mane to its hooves with loca-
vore kale chips, laminated brioches, chanterelle dumplings, and
hand-pulled tripe noodles.

If the pigeons of Battery Park are all former human beings,
the ones that spend all of their time pecking at other pigeons'
grains may well be the avian specters of former investment bankers
driven by an afterworld's abating sense of Supply.

Avenue F, if it existed, would be in the middle of the East River
and would stand for Fathom or Furlong on alternating days. A
sponge able to absorb all of the East River would need to be as
large as the dimenstions of the old Tompkins Square Park bandshell squared and then cubed.

The Hudson is a "blackwater" river,
    dense and impenetrable,
        as if to provide an undulating margin of relief
            after the stark optic assault of Manhattan's streets.

During our most recent Ice Age, the Wisconsin Glacier carved out the fjord that formed the Hudson River, but modern-day Manhattan owes modern-day Milwaukee nothing for that service.

If the water from the Hudson lapping against
    the pilings of Battery Park
        is a well-fed, sonorous baritone;
            the water of the East River clapping against its piers
                is a needling and skeptic soprano.

The upper Manhattan panhandle cannot be used to ladle and sift gold out of the Harlem River any more than the Flatiron Building can be used to press the wrinkles out of Manhattan's collective attire. If our implements were animated by their ingredients instead of their intentions a compass with its needle made out of soft pretzel set loose in Manhattan would slowly, consistently point toward the nearest body of saline water.

As the 20th century loomed near, the shrinkage of Manhattan's open waterfront began to gain on the shrinkage of its passenger pigeon population. On the day of Prohibition's repeal, the bubbling pourage in Manhattan probably rivaled the foaming pourage of Niagara Falls.

As the nature of New York City crime changes, one learns that one can be held up at tongue-point or at eyebrow-point as well as at gun-point. Manhattan is standing proof that there are as many perpetrator-free crimes as there are victimless crimes.

In the dreams of Manhattan's maven class,
    in order to serve as maître d' at now-defunct Elaine's
        or a doorman at the now-departed Hotel Astor
    one needed to possess a rheumatic elbow
        that could predict sudden downpours
    and an arthritic kneecap that could predict upturns
        in class-driven crime.

·｜·╱·｜·╱·｜·╱·｜·╱·｜·╱·｜·╱·｜·╱·｜·╱·

    The task force assembled to solve a crime of fashion replaces its blood-spatter analyst with a sequin-scatter analyst. In Manhattan, the people pressed up against the police barricade surrounding a crime-scene tend to be the most jaded instead of the most curious.

Detection and Enforcement are
    a pair of windshield wipers
        set on "Intermittent"
            during a white-collar crime-storm.

＊｜＊｜＊｜＊｜＊｜＊｜＊｜＊｜＊｜＊｜＊｜＊｜＊｜

    Would Manhattan's borrowing power and credit status be any less vulnerable if it dunked its comptrollers in the East River by their heels and its hedge-fund managers in the Bethesda fountain by their loss-margins?

    Has any over-obsessive art-lover yet connected the elbow-to-knee ratio of Picasso's *Guernica* to the same ratio in the Iwo Jima memorial or the number of lifted feet to planted feet in Matisse's *The Dance* to the average long-distance freeze-frame of the New York City Marathon?

If Manhattan features AAA or XXX train-lines, their destinations are a classified secret beyond the clearance of the average strap-hanger. If waterfront Manhattan sported a representative boardwalk, its planks would alternate between Waldorf walnut, Murray Hill mahogany, Taino teakwood, and Audubon Avenue ebony.

If the 5'2" Fiorello LaGuardia was indeed a "lower-case Franklin Roosevelt," which Manhattan politico was a bold-print Aaron Burr? An Adams in italics? A misprinted Madison? If Madison Avenue is Advertising Alley, which of New York's streets are Bulletin Boulevard, Periodical Promenade, and Gossip Gulch?

□□□□□□□□□□□□□□□□□□□□□□□□□□□□□□□□□□□

If our brains were side-parted like a Navy cadet's hair instead of middle-parted like a riverboat gambler's, Manhattan's think-tanks would have different approaches to certain problems. If an uptown trend is a tide rippling along the pond of a populace, a downtown fad is a dorsal fin cutting through the depths of a demographic.

If a stand-up comedian at one of Manhattan's talent-clubs uses a microphone as a harpoon, the native ghost of Herman Melville winces in his eternal sleep. If a microphone is raised like a torch, Emma Lazarus" specter goes looking for an alibi.

∧∧∧∧∧∧∧∧∧∧∧∧∧∧∧∧∧∧∧∧∧∧∧∧∧∧∧∧∧∧

If a game of chess were played with the thirty-two most famous buildings in the world, would the Empire State building be allowed vertical, diagonal, or linear movements? Would the World Trade Center benefit from a Desperado Sacrifice if Chicago's Sears Tower were capable of a Rook, Hook, and Crook Endgame?

If Wall St. were permitted to rewrite Aesop's fables,
　　their foxes and crows would get upgrades and acquittals
　　　and their lambs would get dressings-down
　　　　and debt-management counselors.

　Wall St. needs beehive markets and matador markets to keep its bear markets and bull markets honest because Wall St. is a galactic golf course with as many black holes as rabbit holes and as many sinkholes as wormholes.

When an iceberg six times the size of Manhattan
　　breaks off from Antarctica,
　　　　Wall St. hires a few more environmental anti-experts
　　　　　and ice-age agnostics
　　　　　　to supplement its Doomsday deniers.

§§§§§§§§§§§§§§§§§§§§§§§§§§§§§§§§§§§§§

　The more fiduciary equivalents of crayon-drawing IOU's and popsicle-stick promissory notes a Wall St. portfolio contains, the closer to collapse it is. A Lennox Avenue Blue Monday and a Wall St. Black Friday optimally keep a St. Patrick's Ash Wednesday in between them at all times.

　In some poetically parallel dimension, negative assets manager leave the opposite of footprints walking down Wall St. in foot-deep snow and the dedication page for the typical memoir of a typical Soho investment banker is so over-brimming with co-conspirators it becomes an "incrimination page" when held up to the noon-light of a power brunch.

Dragonflies are also referred to as "darning needles" because of a folk legend in which they sew shut the eyelids of children. Some appellate court verdicts would seem to suggest that we need a mutant species of dragonfly willing to sew shut the lips of Madison Avenue slanderers and the hands of Wall St. usurers.

Wall St.'s Art Deco architecture:
proof that steel can be galvanized
but marble can only be impressed
and the process of red-brick resurfacing leaves a
fine powder of postponing ellipses and avoided tax-fines.

Charles Dickens was most impressed by Manhattan's "elasticity," but one wonders if Dickens was aware that elastic materials (technically speaking) return to their original form. Since such is the case, Manhattan must surely be among the least elastic places on the planet.

The cogs and gears of the Manhattan engine include
a mid-summer Tompkins Square drum circle and
the revolving doors at Macy's,
the carousel of animal musicians
at the entrance to the Central Park Zoo
and a centrifugal whirlpool spiraling down a Murray Hill sewer.

8888888888888888888888888

Someday a new upheaval of the continental crust may well drive Spear of Destiny-shaped Manhattan in between the waterfront ribs of Red Hook or down the gullet of the Gowanus Canal. At one point, Waverly Place in Greenwich Village intersects itself at an irregular Y-angle indeed resembling a gladiator's spear, as if to protest being named for a Sir Walter Scott novel.

For many, Manhattan is a wish-defying wishing-well
    whose water-surface recedes away from a plummeting penny
    and rises up in a floodtide to swallow a tax rebate whole.

   In New York's urbane and postmodern climate, we trip and
stumble over certain mental and cultural borders because we are
busy showing off how easily we skip and glide over others.

   When pressed to the edge of aphorism, Manhattan is a plum-
met off the precipice of Purpose using a parachute made out of
Potential.

In the Manhattan jigsaw puzzle
    the Columbus Circle pieces don't have round edges
        any more than the Times Square pieces have sharp corners
        and the Hudson waterfront pieces don't have jutting piers
            any more than the St. Patrick's pieces have fluted towers

.:.:.:.:.:.:.:.:.:.:.:.:.:.:.:.:.:.

   If Oklahoma was the epicenter of America's Dust Bowl, Times
Square was once the tornado's eye of its Smut Bowl and Wall St. is
now the axis of its Distrust Bowl. If the taste of its tap-water were a
measure of an area's advancement, New York City would be a lower
Paleolithic outpost with swamp-ferns in every sip.

If pieces of the deconstructed Berlin Wall
        are now being used as ashtrays,
            fragments of the former Ellis Island Reception Center
            will one day be used as lint filters.

If walking from Times Square to Herald Square were an act of intra-national immigration, its passports would need to be rubber-stamped with an icon resembling a shopping-bag and its visas with an icon evoking a bus-transfer.

If Central Park is indeed NYC's lungs, was the Bowery's former Skid Row its kidneys and the Meatpacking District its small intestine? If mice are indeed gnawing away at fiber-optic cables in overhead crawlspaces up and down Wall St., how many million nibbles away from a bubonic-scale monetary brownout are we?

+++++++++++++++++++++++++++++

If Manhattan's coffee intake indeed exceeds most cities' collective water intake, its nervous twitch output suitably dwarfs most cities" deliberate gesture output and its insomnia is more alert than many a small town's main drag at noon.

If, in some inter-borough and occupation-honoring
        version of the afterworld,
transfer-tokens are placed over the eyes
        of deceased train conductors,
plug nickels are placed over the eyes
        of Times Square arcade operators
and commemorative manhole covers
        over the eyes of subway-line excavators.

A suicide leap from a billion Empire State buildings piled vertically would give one enough time to sing a Broadway musical from beginning to end with room for an Art Deco encore. Singing "Mr. Tambourine Man" in reverse will not cause spare coins to fly from the velvet-lined guitar case of a subway busker because donation as a kinetic force tends toward the unidirectional.

That conga line emerging out of a bodega
   and that aerosol can emitting a Jackson Pollock
      are just two of the many Manhattan-induced hallucinations
        that Hollywood is prone to suffering

ßßßßßßßßßßßßßßßßßßßßßßßßßßßßß

If Delancey St. had its own drone missile, its launch code would be a chord sequence from an old Mamas and Papas song. If Manhattan printed its own currency, Duke Ellington would be on the 88-dollar bill.

In some just-concocted Juilliard proverb
   a guitar made out of unraveled screen-door fibers
      can play down-home blues much easier
         than it can play Debussy
            and befriend a jug-bass and a juice-harp
              with greater jubilance.

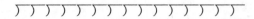

The sound of the square footage of midtown office space being paced off by a pair of stiletto heels is a crucial part of Manhattan's percussion section. The sound of quasi-precious metals being minted out of virtual trades is a crucial part of Manhattan's brass section.

The writer's equivalent of La Monte Young's *Dream House* music (a remotely guided "composition" of sustained pitches droning on toward eternity in an installation space in lower Manhattan) would be a pen guided by a robot hand writing a single sentence with nested phrases ("The man who saw the pigeon who saw the squirrel who saw the ....") ad infinitum...

The sonnet on the plaque at the Statue of Liberty's base was written by a woman whose surname is ironically the name of the Bible's most famous resurrectee. Erase ninety percent of the words in said sonnet and you can still form the phrase "Give me giant-conquering fame, free command, and brazen name."

Alternative poses for the Statue:
　　arms crossed high across the chest a la Run-DMC,
　　　　or index finger to ground like a hunched-over sprinter
　　　　ready to strike,
　　　　　　or left hand waving in jets to LaGuardia
　　　　　　and waving away oil tankers from Venezuela

ロロロロロロロロロロロロロロロロロロロロロロロロロロロ

The broken shackles that the Statue of Liberty stands amid fortunately cannot be re-locked with the mayorally granted keys to the city. The lyrically undulating folds in the statue's toga cannot be pressed smooth by its merciless oxidation from copper to green.

In tribute to its upward-aiming torch,
　　the scraped-clean Statue returns to a fully oxidized green
　　　　at the same rate as Saturn revolves around the sun
　　　　　　and is passed by about as many Staten Island ferries
　　　　　　as Jupiter has confirmed moons every day.

ἀ⪼ἀ⪼ἀ⪼ἀ⪼ἀ⪼ἀ⪼ἀ⪼ἀ⪼ἀ⪼ἀ

Perhaps New York needs to concede that the greatest tribute France ever paid to America was not the Statue of Liberty but naming a Parisian street gang the "Dixie-Fried Hellcats." Perhaps the city also needs to admit that if the book held by the Statue of Liberty featured the word "paradise" and "painless," said words would be "chiseled" in the sense of engraved and "chiseling" in the sense of scamming at once.

In a near-correspondence between commemorative engineering and higher-primate anatomy, the Statue of Liberty originally arrived in New York in 214 separate crates, eight more than there are bones in the human skeleton.

Is the word "trend" going from noun to verb (and "getting" going from verb to noun) any more blame-able on a Madison Avenue martini luncheon than a Wall St. cappuccino summit? Does Plato's "Let no one enter the Academy who is not a geometer" find its contemporary rejoinder in Goldman Sachs' "Let no one enter our break room who is not a differential vector statistician able to bend columns into profit-spigots"?

In terms of urban recoil, what flew further in Jazz Age Manhattan:
a derby blown off by a garlic-induced sneeze in Little Italy,
    a straw boater blown off by a waterfront breeze in Battery Park,
        or a badger-brush fedora blown off
            by a midtown hansom-cab ride?

«±«±«±«±«±«±«±«±«±«±«±«±«±«±«±

In one scriptural account, God the potter forms the rotating earth from the central spindle of the Dome of the Rock. What kind of city would we inhabit if God had begun his spinning from Columbus Circle or the Lincoln Tunnel or used Cleopatra's Needle as his primal axis?

Were more babies born during Manhattan's baptism boom,
    its bar-mitzvah boom, its believers-in-exile boom,
        or its Bible-beating boom?

What anatomic clues does a park-bench performance artist in Tompkins Square give us as to what kind of inaudible music she is dancing to? What auditory clues does she give us as to what invisible supporting cast she is addressing? What kind of intersection can she manage between her non-existent backstage and her perpetually contested fourth wall?

Acousticians refer to the onset of a sound as its "shoulder" :
    in the respective wavecrests of Bronx, Brooklyn,
        and Queens accents,
            which is the broad shoulder, the sloped shoulder,
            and the dislocated shoulder?

In terms of arthropod efficiency, an ant-farm contoured like a scale version of Manhattan's streamlined subway network may be used to deliver a bread-crumb mandible-to-mandible from Battery Park to Inwood Park in record time and with a minimum of pheromone communication.

On one particular summer subway symbol-meter,
    top button undone means "carefree,"
        middle button undone means "careless,"
            and bottom button undone means "uncaring."

+++++++++++++++++++++++++++++++

A disembodied act of diplomacy on the ghost of Duke Ellington's part: since "Take Me Out to the Ballgame" was written on a Manhattan subway, "Take the A-Train" now retroactively claims to have been written in the Polo Grounds bleachers in the name of municipal balance.

    The spinal sway and flex
        required by the pitch and lurch of subway-riding
        is a kind of "situational scoliosis."

Germany names some of its intercity trains for operas, but Manhattan's odd self-effacement still refuses to name its subway cars for Broadway musicals or its municipal buses for legendary Village Vanguard cutting sessions or its aerial tramway to Roosevelt Island for its Lincoln Center ballet premieres.

On an express train,
reading the staccato shouts and hollers of the New York Post
in a clouded overhead mirror
is much easier than reading the sustained analyses
of the Wall Street Journal
over someone else's tweed-encased shoulder.

The likelihood of a diva's dressing room containing a rattan basket full of marzipan fruit increases along the most remote sections of barely-Off-Broadway. Longing for a time when Off-Off-Off-Broadway dress rehearsals turned into undress rehearsals means also longing for a time when being held at knifepoint was cardio exercise. Plant ten additional Off's onto Off-Off-Broadway and you'll be staging a nude revival of Ionesco or Pinter on a wave-battered coral reef in the Long Island Sound.

The subway turnstile that emits two squeaks for every swivel is guilty of mechanical hyperbole. Certain Manhattan subway maps, once unfolded, are equally intent on a purgatory of a puzzle-stage and an origami afterlife.

«±«±«±«±«±«±«±«±«±«±«±«±«±«±«±«±«±

In a figurative lesson drawn from Manhattan's frequently-literal sense of Animal Justice, a T.S. Eliot book about felines being converted into a blockbuster Broadway musical elicits cross-species and cross-town envy from a Westminster Kennel guide to show-dogs.

On Broadway, the difference between an apprentice
     and an understudy
          is often the difference between serving and supplicating
               or between bending over and bowing.

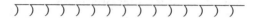

Broadway plays can't deploy extras as massively as Hollywood movies can (because of the load-bearing limits of a stage's floorboards) and so have to "imply" or "evoke" a crowd by means of exaggerations in demographic differential instead.

In between Broadway and Bowery,
     the blind spot between your eyes is filled in by your beliefs,
          the blind spot behind your head is filled in by your biases,
          and the blind spot between your legs is filled in
               by someone else's bawdiness.

If Chelsea had its own flag it would have
     half-fresh tropical produce in place of stars,
          faded bike lanes in place of stripes,
               and a gallery curator holding aloft
                    an implied contract in place of a crest.

If a mummy were ever wrapped inside pages of the New York Times Media and Advertising section, he would wake up with a metropolitan migraine able to shake up a dozen pharaonic dynasties at once.

If five different patients at Bellevue claim to be the reincarnation of Moses, placing them in the same dormitory creates a chamber of echoes, ricochets, mistranslated Aramaic, and commandment postscripts.

If Morningside Heights had its equivalent of Mt. Rushmore,
  it could feature a lichen-covered Jimmy Walker
    and a wind-worn Adam Clayton Powell
      just as easily as an eager-to-avalanche Billie Holiday
        or a Samuel Goldwyn with his hairline festooned
          with transplanted palms.

ꝫʃɑꝫʃɑꝫʃɑꝫʃɑꝫʃɑꝫʃɑꝫʃɑꝫʃɑꝫʃɑꝫʃɑꝫʃɑꝫʃɑʃ

If Manhattan's tap-water emerges from its faucets,
  its flap-water emerges from its arguments,
    and its snap-water emerges from its judgments,
      and its dap-water emerges from its handshakes.

If 42nd St. embodied the 42nd Psalm
  and 5th Avenue paralleled the 5th Commandment,
    would Wall St. or Madison Avenue have to play
the plague-bringing Book of Revelation?

There are linen closets overlooking Columbus Circle whose
hinges cringe at the concept of coin-operated laundromats, and
cedar closets with direct lineages to Lebanon. Local warming is
running neck and neck with global warming, in part because of
the dry-cleaning techniques used north of Columbus Circle and
the idling limousine exhaust between Times and Herald Squares.

Re-moniker and re-metaphor New York as a Big Atom
  instead of a Big Apple
    and the Circle Line ferry tour
      would become one of its electron orbitals
        several media-hubs would compete for an
          uncontestable claim as "nucleus"
            and rapidly emerging and fading micro-barrios
              would serve as quarks.

Seeing Satan's horns in the legs of a compass laying on a city planner's drafting-desk makes it harder to see Columbus Circle as an angel's halo. When one views Manhattan as a vertical text, Columbus Circle can feel like a misplaced comma in the surging syntax of Broadway, or a lower-left asterisk to the block-quote of Central Park.

When Manhattan is feeling one of its periodic extremes
of narcissistic self-regard
it views itself as a circle of cosmopolitan conestoga wagons
on alert for the footfalls of the war-painted upstarts
of Secaucus, Weehawken, and Ho-ho-kus.

००००००००००००००००००००००००००००

Upper East Side housemaids
from the dismantled socialist empires
are more likely to vacuum a carpet
in time-consuming circles
than maids from more capitalistic republics
because pedicab-drivers from Senegal
and rickshaw-operators from Mali
endure an oppressive sense of "around-the-block"
in the Central Park hinterlands.

In another bestial parable from Manhattan's art-world, if an ant-farm modeled after Mondrian's *Broadway Boogie-Woogie* were permitted to devour all of the bread-crumbs left behind by a French Impressionist picnic performed by live actors, the very notion of "cross-genre" would learn a valuable lesson.

According to Manhattan's tonic taste-makers, an egg-cream recipe so esoteric it requires more ingredients than Eggs Benedict would be a betrayal of the blunt and primal effervescence of the egg-cream. According to Manhattan's fiscal pace-makers, New York's history of credit-crunches is a veritable granola, featuring five subprime flake-outs for every over-mortgaged nut and two zero-coupon zest-scrapings for every supply-slanted droplet of housing-crisis honey.

Stage Deli owner Max Asnas was known as the
"Corned Beef Confucius,"
but post-Borscht Belt Broadway
is still in the process of recruiting
a Sour-Cream Socrates,
an Angel-food Aristotle,
and a Pastrami Plato to offset its fall from neoclassical grace.

❊:❊:❊:❊:❊:❊:❊:❊:❊:❊:❊:❊:❊:❊:❊:❊:❊:❊:

In Harlem, so-called "Sugar Hill"'s sweetener-use increasingly supplements its table-sugar with a global cavalcade of coconut sap, Jamaican molasses, Pakistani date-syrup, and Ecuadorian honey. In Little Italy, a loaf of bread's pattern of swirls, crevasses, gnarls and vacuoles forms a Riviera-like relief map illustrating some of the ways in which yeast, air, water, and wheat can interact.

Andy Warhol's 32 *Campbell's Soup Cans* series
seems blissfully unaware
of having one can for each potential human tooth,
two for each pawn in a chess set,
and one-half for each hexagram in the I-Ching
as if its blunt status as a New York commodity-icon
had blinded it to its more numerological
correspondences.

Traditionally, virgins mix the hallucinogenic brew used in vision quests for aboriginal tribespeople, but Alphabet City cocktails tend to be mixed by decidedly less quarantined barmaids catering to a clientele who are seeking Oblivion and not the Ancestors.

At a Hell's Kitchen victory lunch
    Celebrating a hostile corporate takeover,
the lobster-fork of Damocles hangs over the swing-voter's seat
    and a plastic-wrapped Pickle-Spear of Destiny
lays ready to impale his successor
    at the next board of trustees meeting.

Manhattan is the swivel-bucket Ferris-wheel tall enough to view the fall of the Roman Empire and the Advent of the Transnational Corporation at once. Manhattan is the Promised Land with two paraffin-manicured fingers crossed behind its back.

If Jurgen Habermas is correct and "Manhattan is the capital city of the 20th century," it is also the summer home of 3001, the parking garage of Manifest Destiny, and the wastebasket of Utopia. If Manhattan sported an active volcano, we'd need to feed it the occasional paralegal or credit officer to stave off its fury, or a regular diet of equity traders to stave off its dormancy.

:✳:✳:✳:✳:✳:✳:✳:✳:✳:✳:✳:✳:✳:✳:

Manhattan is an orphanage for the uncircumcised and an embassy for the unbaptized, an amusement park for the unconcerned and an unlimited access pass for the unattached. Manhattan is a mirror that knows when mockery is more effective than mimicry and a peephole that knows when a glimpse is more effective than a gander.

Manhattan, as a cross-wired chameleon
        placed on Identity's checkerboard tablecloth,
is considerably more Hispanic
        since San Juan Hill became Lincoln Square
and a bit more Republican
        since Idlewild Airport became Kennedy.

§§§§§§§§§§§§§§§§§§§§§§§§§§§§§§§§§

Flouting all sense of format, Manhattan is a billionaire
        who brown-bags his lunch
as often as it is a freelancer who caters his own firing
a double-jointed diplomat able play offense at an embassy
        and play coy at a consulate
and a gallery of self-reflecting mirrors
        half-able to tell a mirage from a duplication.

Manhattan is in a constant process of "relapidating" what
Time has dilapidated, and one of those rare places where the
1950s weren't the 1960s before-the-fact hangover and payback. In
Manhattan, Cinco de Mayo, the Puerto Rican Day parade, and
Caribana are fully and ardently celebrated but National Explosives
Disposal Day, Bath Safety Day, and Cell Phone Courtesy Month
are merely and duly commemorated.

In Manhattan's Golden Age of Wastrel Bohemia, the slamming
of a Chelsea Hotel door was more likely to knock a Hindu tapestry
than an eviction notice off the wall and the word "hipster" had yet
to sprout its media-burnished patina.

A Chelsea convenience store door-jamb with its ruler installed
upside-down measures its fleeing robbers negatively by how much
shorter than ten feet they are. A Chelsea thrift store's security
camera tends to grow drowsy in direct parallel to its shrinkage of
meaningful inventory.

The hammer-blows and rivet-twists on a Detroit assembly line related to the beats-per-minute of the average Motown dance-track more noticeably than the pigeon-patter of Chelsea related to the chorus of a Brill Building love song.

Chelsea and Soho frequently-but-figuratively lunch together
    to discuss what other names for portions of London
could coherently withstand being exported across the Atlantic
    without being disoriented in the territorial translation.

††††††††††††††††††††††††††††††††††

The guest books at Chelsea art galleries feature as many inde-cipherable scribbles caused by too many almond lattes as they do patrician European surnames featuring a hyphen and an umlaut, and as many aliases based on society columns as they do alibis based on incoming commuter traffic.

In a surrealist take on class warfare
    a debutante in upper Chelsea over-brushing her hair
        by a few hundred strokes
            generates so much static
                she interferes with the Empire State Building's
                radio transmissions.

When Park Avenue develops its own uranium enrichment pro-gram, Brooklyn will turn its few remaining oil derricks into missile silos. Since the Manhattan Project took place in New Mexico, cur-rent odds favor the Bronx Project occurring in New Ecuador and the Queens Project in New Pakistan.

The same person who believes that we refer to "The Bronx"
    but not "The Manhattan"
        because an article is an unnecessary honorific
            must also wonder whether "Queens"
                is a plural or a possessive missing its apostrophe.

###

If Brooklyn is a tick engorged on the blood of Manhattan's bohemian self-massacre, Manhattan is a tapeworm threading its way through the F-train tunnel. Correspondingly, the scratching-off of lottery tickets tends to be more hesitant and diagonal in Manhattan and more frenzied and vertical in Brooklyn.

The five boroughs of New York revisioned as five fingers
    would devolve into an inter-digit power schism
closing into a fist whenever Staten Island rebels
    against its thumbness
gripping a handrail when Brooklyn dons its pinkie ring
    and throwing both hands overhead when Manhattan
does too much pointing.

∫∫∫

All of the testimony every jury in Manhattan was ever told to disregard contains a Staten Island landfill's worth of libel. When protestors throw shoes at New York City politicos, the Manhattan borough president is likely to get a stiletto heel where the Staten Island borough president would get a steel-toed engineer boot.

In latter-day Manhattan, some men choose a best man for their trial separation and place him in charge of bar-crawls and some divorcees choose a maid of dishonor and place her in charge of her un-bridled shower.

What sort of civically overhauling event could cause Governors Island to be renamed Ambassadors Island but leave Liberty Island's name intact and prevent Ellis Island from being renamed Immigrant Island all at once?

Isn't a side-door speakeasy calling itself
Employees Only
a betrayal of Manhattan's long tradition of
genius layabouts, visionary shirkers,
park-bench fakir, and saintly wastrels?

ʒɒʃɒʒɒʃɒʒɒʃɒʒɒʃɒʒɒʃɒʒɒʃɒʒɒʃɒ

How often does a vacuum cleaner left behind by a janitor get mistaken for an untitled readymade exhibit at the Guggenheim, and what level of free admission determines the quality of the critical response it receives? And who is the piecemeal performance artist who keeps taking a large, scalloped bite-mark out of our "Don't Feed the Pigeons" signs?

What is greater and more gradual—the number of semi-sleep positions in the repertoire of the average Eighth Avenue insomniac, the number of price-positions at the recall of the average Canal St. haggler, or the number of non-tiptoe poses in the arsenal of the average Alvin Ailey dancer?

⧣⧣⧣⧣⧣⧣⧣⧣⧣⧣⧣⧣⧣⧣⧣⧣⧣⧣⧣⧣⧣⧣⧣⧣⧣⧣⧣

How many times a week does the "X" formed by a Water St. banker's suspenders" back-straps stand for "Xerox" and how many times a day does the accent-mark formed by his tie-clip elongate an already-too-long vowel?

Depending on their latitude, do some lampposts invite different leans than others because some lobbies attract different loiterers than others? Does a car-horn programmed to play *The Godfather* theme still mean an increase in the prevalence of cufflinks and pinkie rings in one's neighborhood even above and below Little Italy and east and west of Bensonhurst?

The sound of a Ming vase shattering into shards in an Upper East Side penthouse is an alarm bell whetting the ear of divorce lawyers nationwide. The property values all along Central Park ripple like a tsunami-to-be every time a curator marries an esoteric-assets manager.

In Manhattan, potential Joans of Arc have tended to play bass in hardcore punk bands ever since potential Marie Antoinettes started marrying into advertising dynasties and potential Marie Curies began being diverted into careers in high finance.

::

Professional "sniffers" used to arrange marriages based on compatible perspiration, but today's Tribeca sniffers arrange marriages based on credit ratings and liquid assets. Manhattan boasts certain marriages so mixed they cross borderlines of class, chromosome, cuticle contour, and conviction-rate all at once.

Battery Park City pre-nuptial fortune-cookie proverb:
  the man willing to use plane-exhaust to propose marriage
    must be prepared to use railroad flares
      to announce his divorce.

Because Manhattan-set movies of the early 1950's and 1960's tend to feature close-ups of wedding rings at moments of crisis and betrayal instead of at moments of unity and bliss, an "or else" gets appended to a marriage proposal when old-money is playing its ambassador.

In more voguish times, the East Chelsea version of big-game hunting was antiquing with a sniper-scope and the West Chelsea equivalent of sports fishing involved delivering an underpriced upright piano to a 10th floor parlor by crane.

Manhattan Island is a Wagnerian opera of a walk from top to bottom and a sequel-free sitcom pilot of a stroll from side to side. A walking tour of uptown shoe-stores pressed past its price-limit ends up a limping tour just as a walking tour of downtown saloons sent over its sobriety-limit ends up a wobbling tour.

People walk "for" leisure in many places, but in Manhattan people also walk for luxury, leverage, larceny, and latitude. Consequently, some New Yorkers jay-limp or jay-strut or jay-stumble or jay-sashay where others merely jaywalk.

One can walk around town with one's nose in a book, but the truly committed reader walks around with his knees, navel, and nipples in that book as well. Because cloudgazing is a harder prospect in a city of looming towers, curbglancing and crowdglaring and clubscanning have taken up its optical slack.

Among a Manhattan walk's figurative time-zones:
Avenue A Eastern,
Spending-Spree Central,
Martini-Mulling Mountain,
and Plunging Prime Rate Pacific.

Most of New York's crosswalk buttons are non-functional placebos but remain pill-shaped nonetheless. Most of New York's taxi-meters secretively calculate in an alternative currency but display in dollars nonetheless.

A Park Avenue sleepwalker is generally better at navigating around an Eames sofa, an Avenue A sleepwalker better at negotiating around a milk-crate bookcase, and a bodega sleepwalker better at traversing an all-goods-at-once aisle.

Manhattanites know that what can occur in the blink of a midtown manhole cover and what can occur in the blink of a downtown tunnel entrance cannot always be productively compared. Manhattanites know that at certain levels of an intensely uptown negotiation, a flattering ram or a scattering ram is an improvement on a battering ram.

Manhattanites know that in the Darwinism of departments,
    what most crimps the corners of a clerk's cubicle
        most alleviates the east window of an administrator's office.

JJJJJJJJJJJJJJJJJJJJJJJJJJJJJJJJJJJJJJJJJJJJJJJJJJJJJJJJJJJJJJJJ

Manhattanites know that the blueprints for skyscrapers tend more toward the Acquisitive Azure end of the blue spectrum than the Petite Periwinkle. Manhattanites know that the airspace above skyscrapers can be sold for further unfurling, but the Earth's core below a skyscraper can't be sold for further foundation-ing.

Manhattanites know that transit-worker strikes
    cause footwear to evolve,
        while garbage-collection strikes cause nostrils to mature
        and police-union strikes cause weapons-sales to spike.

Manhattanites know in their navigational bones that while East Hampton might feel halfway to Europe to the Wall St. elite, it is barely one-twentieth of the way to Greenland's tundra. Manhattanites know in their geographic guts that while the Harlem, East, and Hudson rivers can feel like moats, New York's sense of "major metropole" doesn't trump the rest of the North American continent's sense of "mainland."

Manhattanites know that the man who designed Central Park sporting the middle name "Law" doesn't necessarily imply that the man who engineered Tomkins Square Park should have the middle name "Unruly" imposed on his tombstone.

In an already-overcrowded Times Square, referring to one's self in the second person or appointing one's self as an objective third party can be regarded as unlawful assembly. Conversely, in an ominously deserted Sheridan Square, a two-person collision can be regarded as a parliamentary quorum.

Neon is a noble gas on the periodic table but an ignoble gas to a Times Square insomniac: what seems less-than-fair under the severe glow of Times Square neon at midnight can seem more-than-just under the high-beams of a meat-packing delivery truck at 4am.

⁛⁘⁛⁘⁛⁘⁛⁘⁛⁘⁛⁘⁛⁘⁛⁘⁛⁘⁛⁘⁛⁘⁛⁘⁛⁘⁛⁘

A game of three-card monte played with a Tarot deck triangulates Times Square's corners every time the Tower card is used to trump a tourist. A game of three-card monte played on a ouija board can overshadow Times Square's LCD billboards by allowing the alphabet to announce its own intentions.

The descending New Year's ball in Times Square
is a slow-motion guillotine
from the prone perspective
of last year's last few minutes.

◻◻◻◻◻◻◻◻◻◻◻◻◻◻◻◻◻◻◻◻◻◻◻◻◻◻◻◻◻◻◻

How long your pupils take to adjust to the darkness of a Times Square movie theater tells us something different about your character than how long your pupils take to adjust to the darkness of an outer-borough aquarium. How long your walking-pace takes to adjust to a Times Square horde tells us something different about your character than how long your speaking-volume takes to adjust to an indoor/outdoor cocktail crowd.

A triple-espresso pipeline runs at juggernaut speed
from the Bronx's Little Italy down to Manhattan's Little Italy,
but a hand-sanitizer pipeline loiters and performs
three additional loops around
always-overcrowded Times Square.

Below Houston St. Manhattan's gridiron system breaks down. as if glaciers of grey-market commerce had snow-plowed its Cartesian coordinates into post-capitalist confetti. In Manhattan, "downtown" is more of a direction than a destination, until it is more of an honorific than an area.

Tribeca, the Triangle Below Canal, may someday be bordered by "Petulant," the Parallelogram East of Thompson, Under Ludlow, and North of Tribeca. The Triborough Bridge was planned by the Biblically named Robert Moses, a man who shattered many of New York's neighborhoods and enclaves into truly "Mosaic" shards with his development projects.

If animism were capable of class animus, the abused and ignored giant aluminum cube standing in front of a downtown corporate headquarters could tranform into a five-ton steel sphere rolling down a corridor of power at quitting time.

Downtown, a trending pair of non-corrective aviator glasses alone cannot turn a customer into a client or a cashier into a curator. Uptown, an vestigial pairing of decorative suspenders and a garrison belt cannot turn a clerk into a case manager or a cubicle into a corner office.

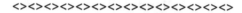

The long lines for uptown copy machines are of a less urgent contour in the age of the electronic attachment. The long lines in downtown post offices are shaped differently—with more slack and with lesser linear tension—since the advent of the cellular telephone and its divertissement.

In terms of relative humility, uptown supermodels don't yet dare to use Cleopatra's waist-to-hip ratio as a personal banking PIN because downtown photographers don't dare to use Leonardo's forearm-to-wrist ratio.

When the Ford Motor Company sponsored television programs it would insist that the Chrysler building be airbrushed out of the Manhattan skyline. When Apple Computer sponsors a television ad, the fruit-carts along Canal St. genuflect in fear. All of the dead air from 1950's live-television broadcasts cannot be used to re-inflate all of the test-balloons that used to hover over Manhattan. All the liquid air used to cryogenically suspend New York's broker elite is an anti-lubricant in terms of class mobility.

When ghosts from different eras of Manhattan's literary history commune at the former site of the Algonquin Round Table, Walt Whitman ignores the finger bowls and Tennessee Williams ignores the drink limits.

When a mayor's assistant is on the witness stand, every greased palm goes sweaty. When a city accountant is under oath, every double ledger gets single-minded. When a pavement-square is upturned into a pup-tent by a poplar root, our engineering science has been deemed superficial by our sub-soil.

When marital arguments break out in Tompkins Square Park, the ghost of the former bandshell becomes a megaphone and the semi-homeless swarm in to volunteer as a binding arbitration committee. In said park, a maple tree lays off its entire work force except for a sap-driving capillary skeleton crew every winter, placing its bark on mute and its leaves on administrative leave.

When Upper West Side waiters are replaced by robots, individual establishments will decide thematically whether to lubricate their elbow-hinges with Mediterranean vinaigrette, hot peanut-oil, or ponzu sauce.

When a downtown Szechuan spice-parlor
    takes the "dump" in "dumpling" too literally
        or emphasizes the "sum" rather than the "dim" in "dim sum"
            taste-buds go on pepper-red alert
                and sweat-glands open their endocrine floodgates.

Central Park's Shakespeare Garden only (deliberately) contains plants mentioned in Shakespeare's dramas and sonnets, but of course "accidentally" plays host to many millions of microscopic and "uninvited" life-forms.

Continental drift cleaved what was eventually South America from what was eventually Africa, but did not pluck Germantown-adjacent Central Park directly from the depths of the Black Forest nor lift the Meatpacking District from the safari zones of the upper Serengeti.

□□□□□□□□□□□□□□□□□□□□□□□□□□□□□□□□□□□

The lights on the Empire State building won't be trained to glow tiger-stripe or leopard-spot to announce escapes from the Central Park Zoo until the Chrysler building agrees to send out searchlights capable of healing Detroit-inflicted holes in the ozone layer…

Central Park is as much an angst–alleviator as it is an oasis
          and as much an idyll-allower as it is an acreage
               and as much avenue-unclogger as it is an Eden.

<><><><><><><><><><><><><><><><><>

Hooverville shanties dotted Central Park during the Depression, but we've since managed to avert Trumantowns, Nixonbergs, and Reaganopoli during our periodic recessions. Soon, wedding vows along both sides of Central Park will be more likely to include the phrases "gross adjusted," "offshore allotment," and "incremental annuity" than lines from Robert Burns or Rumi.

Do the physical gestures that visitors to the Central Park Zoo perform upon departing the primate, bird, and reptile houses indicate that kinesis can recapitulate either phylogeny or ontogeny depending on one's mood? Or that the Darwinian continuum between the species can grow blurrier on a balmy August afternoon?

The "m" and the "n" that form the outer acoustic casing of the word "Manhattan" also form the exact center of the alphabet, as if the borough's name were a Samson pressing two pillars apart with the force of its exhaled vowels. Similarly, the native Lenape word "Mannahatta" seems to possess the same quartet of "a"'s as "amalgamate" for a reason.

"Man-hat-tan" understands the internal rhyme inside the word "adrenaline" just about as well as it does the internal alliteration inside of "momentum." On either side of the Manhattan Bridge, factories convert into residences much more than vice versa, though an investment banker's townhouse paid-for by an unpredictable casino economy could be turned into a fortune-cookie manufacturing plant if poetic justice and economic justice could ever agree on a merger.

∧∧∧∧∧∧∧∧∧∧∧∧∧∧∧∧∧∧∧∧∧∧∧∧∧∧∧∧∧

The uptown 911 call that can afford to use the word "allegedly" has prioritized itself below the downtown 911 call that can't resist using the word "repeatedly." The crosstown ambulance-siren that resembles a moan of pain has less veto-power than the avenue-barreling ambulance-siren that resembles a war-cry.

The dropped "r"'s in a certain kind of Manhattan accent
cannot issue a pronunciation promissory note
nor seek asylum in an eloquence embassy.

ꙄᄼᄼᎯᄼᎯꙄᄼᎯᄼꙄᄼᎯᄼꙄᄼᎯᄼꙄᄼᎯᄼꙄᄼᎯꙄᄼᎯᄼꙄᄼ

The tractor-exhaust needed to grow the components of an organic Waldorf salad in the Waldorf Hotel is sufficient to spell out the word "conundrum" in lingering vapors. The carbon footprint of an Eggs Benedict served at Delmonico's sinks ever-deeper into the composted loam of New York history.

In terms of videocracy, the old rabbit-ear aerial antenna atop an oak-encased color console on the Upper West Side formed a V that served as a monogram for a different word than the V formed by the antenna taped atop a Spanish Harlem bodega's black-and-white.

If a game of chess were played with New York's best-known financial-district landmarks, checkmating would involve check-kiting as surely as each endgame would entail arbitration.

If Manhattan's self-chauvinism could decree it,
    virtual shoplifting and lunch-break jaywalking
      would be Olympic sports judged
        by placard-wielding grand juries.

If Wall St. managed to land its own lunar rover on the moon it would claim that the core samples it collected constituted a new currency and would plant an unlimited-license land-deed instead of a flag.

If an Iron Curtain divided capitalism and communism,
    a Bamboo Curtain separates Canal St. from Wall St.,
      a Petticoat Curtain separates Madison Avenue from Macy's,
        and a Rayon Curtain separates our design houses
          from our sweatshops.

<><><><><><><><><><><><><><><>

If a criminal suspect is a "person of interest" and a homeless man is a "person of disinterest," a downtown banker is a "person of intensely compounded interest." If bankers search online for ways to quit drinking on Thursdays more than Mondays, they presumably shop for parkas in August more than in April and for sleep-masks more at apprehensive dusk than bleary-eyed dawn.

If America's main patent office were located in Manhattan instead of Washington D.C., would a gadget able to convert spare nickels into special-purpose asset swaps be protected by now? If Manhattan's utility lines are its arteries and its storm-sewers are its intestines, which public monument is its gallstone and which traffic jam is its diverticulitis?

Humankind discovered fire by rubbing hard-woods and soft-woods together, music by rubbing hard sounds and soft sounds together, and Wall St. by rubbing hard currencies and soft currencies together. There are tax boondoggles being developed up and down Wall St. with more pivots, twists, and switchbacks than the most gnarled and deflected stream in upstate New York.

In post-Einstein Manhattan, is the "speed" of currency--when we factor in all of the pinwheel conversions, triple-axel differentials, and zero-inverse somersaults it performs--indeed faster than the speed of light?

«±«±«±«±«±«±«±«±«±«±«±«±«±«±«±

A rolled-up edition of the Wall Street Journal can serve as a diviner's wand where a rolled-up copy of the New York Post can only serve as a cudgel because certain Social-Darwinist oral supplements imbibed on Wall St. are said to cause attention-surplus disorder.

Does a swivel-back office chair
    in a West Village accountant's office
        rotate 720 degrees before making a questionable decision
    that an executively ergonomic chair on Wall St.
        could have managed in a mere 90?

Wall St. is a bare-fanged barracuda tank masquerading as a remedial calculus class and a koi pond pretending to be Fort Knox. On the casino-finance playing field, a game of getting even requires a gridiron made of Revenge, a goalpost made of Resentment, and a golf-club made of Remorselessness.

As a Times Square scarf vendor's inventory stagnates, his clearance-sale cart begins lubricating its own getaway axle. As a Canal St. knockoff counterfeiter's vision dims, his ability to spell designer names begins to scramble for cover.

The tip-jar at a Union Square bistro accepts coins, rejoices at bills, and grimaces at tokens. The interrogative "Why Pay More?" placard hung in a neighboring discount-store window doesn't allow responses drawn from *Das Kapital,* the Tao Te Ching, or the Gospel of St. Mark for three very different reasons.

A Manhattan business district birdwatcher's guide that was true to the spirit of its locale would feature a turkey-vulture center-fold and freelance-raptor classified ads and a bird-of-prey personals section.

Manhattan has four discount-store taste-breakers for every Madison Avenue tastemaker. Hardware stores in Soho sell more papier-mâché than hammers because art-supply stores in Bensonhurst sell more screwdrivers than paint-brushes.

The family crest of a newly anointed
    Chambers St. discount-store dynasty
        features a personal latte dispenser
            superimposed over an angora scarf
        fluttering in the propwash of a condo-board helipad.

Given a choice in sectarian vandalisms, some stores in Manhattan would prefer having a brick from the Great Pyramid of Cheops thrown through their main window, others a tide-polished pebble from the Jordan River.

Sometimes New Orleans Mardi Gras "go cup" looks for idiomatic comrades like a "loiter-liter" or a "tarry-tankard" to socialize with. Sometimes an elitist Manhattan martini-glass renders its own stem ever-slimmer to minimize its contact with its surroundings.

In Broadway's prop calculus, is the ratio of top hats to martini shakers in a Noel Coward musical close to the ratio of half-slipped suspenders to broken bourbon bottles in a Eugene O'Neill play? Is Manhattan's collective hate-mail better spelled but more bitterly enunciated than the Bronx's, or just more appended with summonses?

Since Manhattan's Freedom Tower stands a "symbolic"
    1,776 feet tall:
What sort of Manifest Destiny museum should be built
    to stand at 1,492 feet tall?
What kind of Anglophobe emporium should aim for 1,812?
What type of Pacific-facing monument should register 1,941?

≳∂≳∂≳∂≳∂≳∂≳∂≳∂≳∂≳∂≳

How would Lincoln Tunnel Vision differ from Holland Tunnel Vision? Which one would associate gridlock with glaucoma and which one would confuse cataracts with catacombs? If certain tribes buried their suicides at the crossroads, what sort of demises should New York City bury at its cloverleaf overpasses or underneath its passing lanes?

The classical Greeks claimed that a wreath of ivy worn around the head would prevent drunkenness induced by wine. What kind of vegetation would one need to wear around one's head to prevent drunkenness induced by a rye cocktail mixed in the Carlyle Hotel?

⠀⠄⠂⠄⠂⠄⠂⠄⠂⠄⠂⠄⠂⠄⠂⠄⠂⠄⠂⠄⠂⠄⠂⠄⠂⠄⠂⠄⠂

A too-regulated Manhattan office manager's deepest REM sleep might well reveal a ratio between the number of Fiorello LaGuardia postage stamps that have been cancelled and the number of LaGuardia Airport flights that have been cancelled, or some other correspondence dug out from the over-fertile loam of urban legend.

In some half-cooked Manhattan spy manual,
    the ingredient in a Waldorf salad
        most likely to conceal a listening device
            depends on the ingredient in Eggs Benedict
most capable of lubricating a microcassette recorder's spindles.

Some smaller villages boast a volunteer fire department or ambulance corps, but New York City has always sported an over-supplied volunteer legion of art critics. These critics know that a museum-goer trying to outstare a woman portrayed by de Kooning and then a woman portrayed by da Vinci is engaging in two very different retinal enterprises.

The spiral ramp to the Guggenheim museum, if uncoiled,
    would span as tall as the average depth of the Hudson River
        times Manhattan's annual snowfall times its annual rainfall
        times the prescribed height of its standard air shaft.

There are six museums devoted to the culture of kimchi in Korea but not a single one devoted to ballpark sauerkraut, Waldorf-destined walnuts or Benedict-destined bacon in New York City. A Museum of Unnatural History would feature dioramas made from Dacron and galleries devoted to gabardine.

The security guards at MOMA "exhibit" varying degrees of Pollock-paralysis, Oppenheim-indifference, and Koons-contempt to supplement the Picasso-passion and Brancusi-belaboring exhibited by tour guides torn between being a
     docent and a debutante.

Stored paintings lean with the self-approving attitude of a street hustler in MOMA's basement but with the anguish of a gall-stone sufferer in the Met's basement. Stored sculptures stand with the stoicism of a neoclassic pantomime at the Whitney and with the serene asceticism of a bodhisattbva at the Rubin.

Perpendicular to the equation above, the blue whale suspended by piano-wires from the rotunda ceiling at the Museum of Natural History sports a grin as wide as the FDR's outside lane and an eye-ball as large as an Upper West Side limousine's spare tire.

The word "conductor" applied to a subway's captain-at-arms and the word "conductor" applied to an orchestra leader only come into class conflict when a baton disagrees with a brake-lever. A train-conductor's relationship with her microphone can be as narcissistic as a cabaret singer's or as fervent as an auctioneer's or as bored as a loading-dock manager's, all on a single trip.

The fewer tool-boxes one sees in the subway,
    the less autonomous a city's growth.
The fewer double-basses one sees in a subway,
    the more automated a city's music has become.
The sparser the crowd in a subway car,
    the more revealing the pattern of seats-chosen.

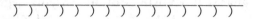

The proportion of pigeons to persons in New York City
    is similar to the ratio of rats to daily subway riders
        but both are unrelated to the ratio
            of half-abandoned fast food to seagulls
            and oblivious to the ratio between
                pet-supply stores and squirrel nut-storage.

    Just as commercial jets can seem slow beyond imagining
and fast beyond comprehension at once, a subway car can seem
overcrowded and alienated to alternating blinks of disbelief and
re-belief.

    When one is thirsty enough one can smell water—when one is
lost enough in the West Village one can smell the mortar between
its cobblestones harkening back to its colonial formation and hear
the clank of its manhole covers being initially fitted into place.

In the Golden Age of the Token,
    a New York subway ride cost a nickel
from the naming of Times Square
    and the sinking of the steamboat Slocum in 1904
to the death of Babe Ruth
    and the opening of the Fresh Kills landfill in 1948.

Does the American 20th Century owe Manhattan more
assistance-credits than it does to any other single place, despite
post-colonial Boston and Philadelphia's willingness to dou-
ble-team? If a Memorial Day parade runs along Broadway, what
byway would most suitably host an "Amnesia Day" pacifist protest
bent on gluing ticker-tape back together?

What kind of oblique justice is pandered to
    if New York City loses a square inch of window-box arugula
        for every acre of rainforest lost in Brazil
           and gains a thousand puffs of taxi-exhaust
for every square inch of ozone layer thinned around our planet?

              ▢▢▢▢▢▢▢▢▢▢▢▢▢▢▢▢▢▢▢▢▢▢▢▢▢▢▢▢▢▢▢▢▢▢

Is the U.N. Building's bland geometric bloodlessness indeed
a gesture toward an International Style or an overcompensation
for it being erected on the former "Blood Alley," a complex of
cow-butchering stockyards?

Who blinks first and who uncrosses his ankles last
    and who clears his throat first and cracks his knuckles last
        when an investment banker tells a lie
           he borrowed from a tax-attorney
               to mislead a hedge-fund manager
                  into a devil's triangulation?

              ∧∧∧∧∧∧∧∧∧∧∧∧∧∧∧∧∧∧∧∧∧∧∧∧∧∧∧

Why are classic old free-standing Murray Hill bathtubs claw-
footed like a water-avoiding cat instead of web-footed like a
water-loving duck? What kind of parallel convergence has been
proven if the average bulletproof Plexiglas taxicab partition has as
many holes-for-talking-through as there are intersections in the
Theater District?

How high would an archaeologist's eyebrows be raised if the cave art in some discontinued subway tunnel in the Upper East Side did not depict hunting parties chasing down bison but rather portrayed debutante pajama parties hunting down worm-spun silk?

New York once suffered under an ex-vaudevillian mayor who composed a popular song titled "There's Music in the Rustle of a Skirt" but who also had a keen ear for the forbidden harmonics in the rustle of a paper-money bribe.

Because of Manhattan's relative lack of room for McMansions, it suffers a proliferation of McMoney, McMandates, McManagements, and McMargins. Because the human digestive tract is an engine of conversion, a Central Park dirty-water hot dog rolls as it floats in its cart-reservoir with the same basic motion as a pine-log en route to a sawmill.

```
*********************************
*********************************
```

The junior stockbroker paying rent to sleep on an off-duty medical-office examination table is incarnating a special blend of Avarice, Adaptability, Abnegation, and Optimism. Many of New York's fiscal better-offs got that way by flouting moral and legal better-not's.

There may be a piano in a penthouse in the Upper East Side with one black key wired to the Pentagon and one to a secret Swiss bank account and one to a petroleum broker that can't have any of its white keys struck without triggering civil war in Venezuela.

.:.:.:.:.:.:.:.:.:.:.:.:.:.:.:.:.

The engineer/investor driving a doomed-to-fail hedge fund
   off of its terminal cliff
      is engaging in a personal program of Planned Pariah-hood
         and sharpening the apex of a plummeting pyramid
            to the point of Ponzitude.

Manhattan features almost as many over-documented heiresses as it does undocumented immigrants and as many infra-documented virtual files as inter-documented tax shelters. Try to extradite a tax-exile out of a Vesey St. fern-bar and said tavern will turn independent embassy in the blink of amnesty's most easily dilated aperture.

The Canal St. trifecta: buying a Fibonacci-rinded pineapple five workdays away from ripeness, a limited-edition purse whose edition is only limited by its factory not being raided, and a Tibetan prayer-flag willing to flutter in Soho's secular crosswinds.

All along Canal St., there is an invisible sales catch to practically every audible sales pitch. The zirconium mines being excavated under Canal St. are giving the sequin mines under Amsterdam Avenue a run for their pocket-money.

«±«±«±«±«±«±«±«±«±«±«±«±«±«±«±«±«±

Latter-day Chinatown isn't encouraged that Henry Hudson "discovered" Manhattan while looking for a shortcut to China any more than latter-day Little Italy is discouraged that Christopher Columbus would have regarded himself as Genoan more than Italian.

Haggling over prices with a Chinatown fruit-vendor
    can go lateral or diagonal as well as vertical
        depending on the fruit-in-question
            and the next day's temperature-in-waiting.

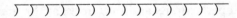

A Canal St. pedicab cycler's calves often seem as large around as the fireplugs he double-parks alongside, in a case of hypertrophy matching hydraulics. A Canal St. rickshaw-hauler's deltoids can seem as broad across as the covered-over canals the street is named for, in a case of development matching disappearance.

The block-long Spice Route between Little Italy and Chinatown is like a track-and-field triple jump consisting of a horseradish hop, a saffron skip, and a juniper-berry jump able to connect two enclaves with herbs and two spending-circuits with seasonings.

Sometimes New York City's name-recognition is crowded out by its numerical notoriety on stock-exchange scoreboards across the globe. Sometimes partisan city politics can be so piecemeal that they can pull a single voter into separate precincts and shred a single ballot into special-interest confetti.

Sometimes New York City is a Doppler Effect
    drawn out across decades
        and a dime-novel aspiring to dollar status,
            and sometimes it is a taffy-pull tug-of-war
          late for its dental appointment
and a tractor-pull looking for its reverse gear and its spare tire.

****
****

Someday a Manhattan millionaire's next-to-last will and testament will be so contested it will be subdivided into a demi-dollar for every resident along the Atlantic seaboard. Someday ebb-tide Manhattan will find itself located figuratively in between Martha's Vineyard's most sour grapes turning to vinegar and a too-promiscuous pickpocket realizing that he owns the world's largest collection of lint.

Sometimes the federal wiretap installed on a St. Patrick's confessional booth perks up its auditory nerve at the mere mention of the phrase "slush fund" and plugs its ears with quaking fingers at the vaguest allusion to "counter-surveillance" and yawns wide at the vaguest hint of "charity ball."

Sometimes the bubble-lettering of outdated East Harlem graffiti looks like it is a police pin-prick away from deflating into a drained zeppelin. Sometimes a police lineup can be so overeducated it turns into the makings of a senate subcommittee, and someday that procedure will be made reversible.

Sometimes a barely raised eyebrow or a self-bitten lower lip is as close as a disaffected Manhattanite can come to genuflecting or bowing in awe. Sometimes a fear-furrowed brow or a half-stiff upper lip is as close as an overexcited Manhattanite can come to full-body impulse control.

Observant Manhattanites know that the zodiac ceiling of Grand Central's main concourse has an ironic stain caused by cigarette smoke located at the constellation of Cancer. Manhattanites knew before most that the checkerboard floor of a 1950's suburban kitchen was there to remind wives of their pawn-hood and husbands of their knave-hood, unlike the checkerboards of a Little Italy tablecloth or a taxicab's doors.

At birth, Manhattanites are implanted
   with a Collision Avoidance System,
      a nerve-end sonar attentive to fellow pedestians
     at crosswalk cross-purposes
    and a hormonal apparatus that can be switched off
     at key moments of confrontation.

⅏ ⅏ ⅏ ⅏ ⅏ ⅏ ⅏ ⅏ ⅏ ⅏ ⅏ ⅏ ⅏

Manhattanites know that in between Paradise Lost and Paradise Regained come Paradise Negatively Mortgaged, Paradise Liquidated, and Paradise Publicly Auctioned. Manhattanites also know that if the face of a Catholic saint can appear in the scorchmarks on a Spanish Harlem tortilla, then logically the multiple arms of a Hindu deity can appear in the spill-pattern overflowing a Curry Hill clay pot and the genitals of Bacchus can appear in a cluster of grapes in a Little Italy bistro.

Manhattanites know that if Cloud 9 is untrammeled ecstasy,
Cloud 8 is a tremor of anticipation,
Cloud 10 a rueful hangover,
Cloud 11 is resumptive dusting one's self off
and moving along,
and Cloud 12 a new lease on libido.

⁜:⁜:⁜:⁜:⁜:⁜:⁜:⁜:⁜:⁜:⁜:⁜:⁜:⁜:

Few Manhattanites are inclined to allow the borough's Cartesian geometry to hem in their social strivings. Some Manhattanites prefer being diagonally mobile dilettantes to being upwardly mobile strivers. All Manhattanites know that there are acquired distastes as well as acquired tastes.

As stereotypically born aggressors and uprooters, Manhattanites
tend to prefer
the boxer who ends rounds furthest away from his own corner
the baseball slugger most prone to splinters
and the soccer striker most willing
to shred his jersey into souvenirs.

Upper East Side exceptionalism is based on an ego-principle that cannot afford to integrate with Manhattan's mass-movement mongrelismo. As summer camps named for Indian tribes are eclipsed by camps named for donors seeking tax write-offs, Upper East Side parents undergo the transition from occupiers-of-the-aboriginal to recipients-of-royal-welfare.

On an Upper East Side elevator,
     a depressive standing in front of an optimist
         standing in front of a paranoid
forms an unfolded huddle,
     a status-quo queue,
         and a bipolar eclipse.

ЖЖЖЖЖЖЖЖЖЖЖ

A form of malaria transmissible by teacup poodles instead of
mosquitoes and a species of gout inflamed by blood-pressure
medication rather than instant ramen would both turn the Upper
East Side into a gumbo-dense fever-swamp.

    The clatter and tinkle of medic-alert badges provide a bed
of percussion at early-bird Upper East Side bistros that resonates
and rattles like a geriatric xylophone under a hailstorm of salad-
bar contortions.

ৠৠৠৠৠৠৠৠৠৠৠৠৠৠৠৠৠৠৠৠ

    An Upper East Side dog-walker works from a radial octopus
stance and gives more frequent yanks on the chain to Alsatians
and more encouraging words to Pomeranians. The abort code for
an Upper East Side home invasion can be "faux-diamond" but can
also be "Doberman."

On certain stretches of overrefined Upper East Side,
     the aerosol canister of the Ego
         is eating away at the ozone layer of the Id
            at an increment rate of inches per instinct.

If one could walk with a portable electrified fence around one's personal space, Manhattan's wariness and wattage would both increase correspondingly. If old Route 66 had ever bisected Manhattan, our domestic sense of a "continental" breakfast would be different and our idea of West-of-Hudson more porous and inclusive.

If Manhattan were to become a literal ghost town,
    upper Central Park would be as haunted
        by the specters of disappeared dog-walkers
        as lower Central Park would be
            by the phantoms of forgotten pretzel-vendors.

«±«±«±«±«±«±«±«±«±«±«±««±«±«±«±

If Foley Square were turned into Foley Circle, would Inwood be encouraged to go isosceles and Riverside Park risk going rhomboid and Time-Warner be tempted to go trapezius?

If single male subway riders' pupils do indeed constrict at a squalling infant, does the smell of sanitized and prophylactic rubber cause those same pupils to re-dilate?

If acronyms begin to assemble single-file
    whenever federal funds flow into Manhattan,
        the taking-over of a condo board in slow motion
can resemble a team of termites reducing a banister to sawdust.

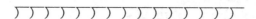

If every grease fire incurred while preparing Eggs Benedict goes on Manhattan's rap sheet, every Broadway musical finalized over Lobster Newberg and every worry evaporated into a Bloody Mary go into its parole recommendation.

If lower Manhattan were half-converted into a wildlife reserve, "Don't Feed the Corporate Bond Manager" signs would outnumber "Don't Take Anything But Pictures, Don't Leave Anything But Footprints" signs.

The receipts at midtown franchise stores are long enough to mummify a deposed pharaoh and come faded enough to strain the optic acuity of a Zen archer's monocle. A Mafia bookkeeper witness relocated to midtown Manhattan develops a crick in his neck as complex as one of Einstein's preparatory calculations.

A cologne trying to evoke midtown Manhattan
        would have to balance
                its summer sandal-wood with idling and ozonic
                    diesel fumes
                        and the top-note hints of burnt-out signage
                            with the inessential oils
                                of rain-damp theater programs.

✿✿✿✿✿✿✿✿✿✿✿✿✿>

Dangle an adhesive anti-pest strip from a roof-beam of a midtown deli and it will occasionally attract flies in the pattern of the sheet music to a post-1945 Broadway show-tune. Try to maintain ownership of a gull-wing racing car in midtown Manhattan and it quickly becomes a white elephant with a peanut allergy and an albatross around one's Ego.

When a midtown deli starts naming its sandwiches
    for hedge-fund managers,
        it will need to name a pickle after a particular pyramid scheme
            and a hot mustard after a tax haven in the Antilles.

If Manhattan —
    the dribble-glass of data overload drowning on itself —
    had an Outwood to balance its Inwood
        it would need two polar Endtowns
            for its magnetic Midtown to separate.

Since Manhattan's antipode of Perth, Australia
    has named its tallest building "Central Park,"
New York City owes its sister city a building named for Ayers Rock
    and a park-ramble more Outback than Arden.

In Tribeca foot-traffic, au pairs wield baby-carriages like scud missiles and synchronize their stopwatches as well as their score-cards. In Tribeca, an especially privileged adolescent's "paper route" consists of land-leases, title bonds, and self-correcting contracts.

What would depopulate Tribeca fastest —
    an edamame famine, a free-range ostrich-meat blockade,
or a Riesling drought — depends on virtue-signaling embargos
    as well as vice-dependent tariffs.

::

In Tribeca, house-calls will one day be expected from ris-ing-waterfront alleviators, kayak guides, and Esperanto tutors. In that same Tribeca, the velvet rope that separates the rarefied from the rabble will be the serpent in the Garden of Elitism.

On the frayed corners of Tribeca's social register,
    keeping up with the Kennedys is often less pleasurable
than pulling a takeover of the Parkinsons
    undercutting a merger of the Moodys
        or falling out with the Fitzgeralds.

Inner-circle Tribeca is often the bugle blowing a ragtime-syncopated version of "Taps" over the carcass of ten minutes ago's failed efforts at a trend or the trumpet that calls global capitalism to attention.

Tribecans know that even the best hedge fund can't buy a suburban hedge tall enough to block out all evidence of your neighbors nor deeply rooted enough to ensure you of your own private tapwater.

The Laissez-Faire Land-Grant:
Where Manhattan's so-called Silk Stocking District never called the Tenderloin the "Black Fishnet District" despite sufficient cause.

The Warding-off Ward:
Where putting a lobby in front of an antechamber in front of a vestibule in front of a foyer makes an inner sanctum practically un-enterable.

The Protean Zone:
Where an overuse of the hybridizing "slash" allows a single room to become an activist printshop/performance space/yoga center/juice bar and a Brooks Brothers three-piece to become a uniform/costume/suit of armor/disguise.

****
****

The Historical Conundrum Corridor:
Where Hudson Heights is part of Washington Heights (and not vice versa) despite Hudson the Explorer having paved the way for Washington the Warrior.

The Promo-dome:
Where the volume and cadence of talk at a West End singles bar turns everyone into a self-auctioneer, a self-docent, a self-marketer, and a self-stylist at once.

The Quid Pro Quo Quarter:
Where what happens behind a slammed-closed door and what happens behind a too-gently-closed door are interrelated political entities.

ʃɑꙄɑʃɑꙄɑʃɑꙄɑʃɑꙄɑʃɑꙄɑʃɑꙄɑʃɑꙄɑʃɑꙄɑʃɑ

The Density District:
Where a zipcord run between two buildings on either side of a street is often a zipcord between zip codes as well.

Atavism Alley:
Where many of our Stone Age paleo-behaviors re-emerge when we are left alone in a sparsely furnished postmodern condo for too long.

Manhattan knows that there are performance-anxiety artists as well as performance artists. The artist five years ahead of his time and five installments behind on his easel payment and five minutes late for his fifteen minutes of fame always seems to need five swipes for his transit-pass to take.

Despite its art-world preeminence,
    New York City is yet to have sponsored a fireworks display
        featuring a rocket shaped like a Rauschenberg,
            an air-bomb resembling an Arp,
                a blockbuster modeled on a Brancusi,
                    or confetti-cannon evoking a Calder.

❁❁❁❁❁❁❁❁❁❁❁

A police sketch-artist in a certain zip code of lower Manhattan may have more Braque than Hopper in his wrist. Some graffiti artists "bomb," but some merely "needle," depending on issues of placement, timing, and aggression-to-acrylic ratio.

Downtown Manhattan knows all too well
   why the capitalized "Dow" in "Dow Jones"
    and the uncapitalized "dow"
     in "National Endowment for the Arts"
    generally refuse to overlap

❑❑❑❑❑❑❑❑❑❑❑❑❑❑❑❑❑❑❑❑❑❑❑❑❑❑❑❑❑❑❑

The "cure" will go out of "curator" when the robot arms of a downtown sanitation truck are allowed to paint their first recognized self-portrait with the rainbow tints of an oil-spill. Manhattan knows all-too-well that sometimes an artwork is so untitled its anonymity is an act of aggression.

The "El"'s in "El Barrio" and in "Elevated Train" are frequently on intimate-if-rancorous terms that Manhattan's claim to "inner borough"-hood cannot understand. The graffiti murals that used to ride subway cars into Manhattan from the outer boroughs were rainbow-alert messages to the city's nerve center.

In a wishful-visualizing food-trope, Manhattan's various sub-populations are like separate pizza slices pointing inward toward a common center and not a breadcrumb trail spiraling outward from a hollowed-out crust.

In Depression-era Manhattan,
   soup-lines didn't flow any more fluidly than breadlines
    because breadlines didn't crumble any more piecemeal
    than soup-lines.

The Washington Heights window-boxes currently growing spices for menudo contain enough fixed nitrogen to fuel a space-capsule named the Santo Domingo. The number of salt-crystals studding a single soft pretzel may well approximate the number of pretzel vendors in Manhattan itself without impacting the sodium content of either the city or its sweat-glands.

The faucets labeled Champagne and Malt Liquor
can only be turned on at the same time
in certain especially limber and eclectic parts of town.

⋮⋰⋮⋰⋮⋰⋮⋰⋮⋰⋮⋰⋮⋰⋮⋰⋮⋰⋮

The copepod crustaceans
that float in Manhattan's drinking water
render it microscopically non-kosher
and fractionally anti-halal at once.

During a Fulton St. fish-feud,
unfurling all five fingers from a fist
into a fan forfeits your fury,
just as unfurrowing all five folds from your forehead
forsakes your frown.

If Manhattan Island were a sentence depicting the entire span of human history, would Union Square would be a comma following the declaration of the French and Indian Wars or Columbus Circle be the middle dot in an ellipsis between the Magna Carta and the Reign of Terror? If the 20th century were indeed born in Manhattan, precisely which of its Native-named suburbs were its teething and its toilet-training outsourced to?

What kind of fast food served in New York is most responsible for our bodies now taking longer to decompose once we die and how should this change the meaning of a "Preservation Committee"?

If the act of eating brine-cured tongue at an uptown deli had an "opposite" (either kinetically or existentially), is it too anatomically disturbing to consider what that act might look like? If skyscrapers are indeed streets stood up on end, is the Sixth-Avenue equivalent of a land speed record an elevator race?

In terms of subliminal association,
does Manhattan see the terminal "y" in "New York City"
as a potential slingshot, a fork in Fate's main road,
or a miniature human with its assistance-seeking arms extended?

⚸ ⚸ ⚸ ⚸ ⚸ ⚸ ⚸ ⚸ ⚸ ⚸ ⚸ ⚸

Along Park Avenue, is it more likely for a purse-held Pomeranian to be trained to yip like the jingle of loose change or a teacup poodle be trained to howl like a boiling kettle? Does a crossing guard at a private kindergarten for future Wall St. kleptomaniacs dare to use his "stop" hand more frequently than he uses his "go" hand without the fear of an accusation of overregulation?

Have fruit flies learned not to abandon Canal St. for an uptown exhibit of Cezanne apples or Matisse lemons by developing their own brand of ontological skepticism and realism? Among NYU sophomores, do Maoists button their shirts to the top button in the name of solidarity because would-be anarchists leave their bottom button undone in the name of indiscipline?

In an urban populace a tad too proud of its own mortal survival: soul survivors in St. Patrick's confessional booth, role survivors in a Broadway deli, stole survivors in a Lexington Avenue fur-store, and dole survivors in a crosstown welfare office queue.

The handprints put in the wet cement
in front of a Broadway theater
can't be joined together in self-applause
any more than the Footprints Café can kick up its own heels
or the Village Voice can clear its throat.

ŧ«ŧ«ŧ«ŧ«ŧ«ŧ«ŧ«ŧ«ŧ«ŧ«ŧ«ŧ«ŧ«ŧ«ŧ«ŧ«ŧ

The Broadway actor who won't eat limp noodles before playing a mastermind or vegetables before playing a comatose patient
should analogically also avoid tropical umbrella drinks before playing a chronic depressive or barbecue before playing a burn victim.

.

Off-off-off- Broadway intepretive-dance exercise:
pantomime what it would look like
to rub the daily routine of a stockbroker
against the hourly habits of a hospice care-giver
until the friction breaks out into vocational flames.

ʔʔʔʔʔʔʔʔʔʔʔʔʔʔʔʔʔʔʔʔʔʔʔʔ

Broadway's neon runs on halal-vendor grillowatts
and lost-tourist millowatts
and common starling trillowatts
as well as Mount Sinai outpatient pillowatts.

Broadway is allowed to wander and deviate
from Manhattan's grid system
like an avenue gone AWOL
or a thoroughfare with inexact change.

A Riverside Park squirrel rotates a prospective piece of food in
its paws half as many degrees as a Lennox Avenue jewel appraiser
does a ruby. The mockingbirds that populate the Tree of Peace and
Unity at the UN building have a vast array of accents, dialects,
limousine-horns and dial-tones to imitate.

A brief list of just some of New York's extinct species:
the McSorley's Mastodon,
the Peace Eye Bookstore Pleistocene Fern,
and the Idlewild Egret.

□□□□□□□□□□□□□□□□□□□□□□□□□□□□□□□□

The two beavers on the seal of the City of New York are facing the knickerbocker-sporting Dutchman and not the loincloth-sporting Native for partisan reasons that don't need to be explained but do need to be acknowledged.

The tiger-skin rug in the mayor's office is frozen in a mid-snarl that ominously mirrors the most commonly photographed facial expression of the protesters who occasionally swarm City Hall's lawn.

Manhattan's sanitation workers refer to maggots as "disco rice" but haven't yet found a substance they can call "mosh-pit menudo" or "post-St. Patrick's parade penicillin."

Once the passenger pigeon is resurrected
via fossilized DNA prints,
the resurrection of the Ellis Island taxi dancer,
the Carnegie Deli kibitzer-in-chief,
and the Polo Grounds groundskeeper
won't be far behind.

If attack dogs on the Upper West Side wear stud collars mounted with De Beers poison-tip diamonds, it is because the dolls given to the daughters of hedge-fund managers have eyes that roll back in their heads at the very mention of a non-private prep academy.

If the Dewey Decimal System dictates the arrangement
    of library books,
        the DiMaggio Decimal System arranges
        New York Yankees
            and the D'Amato Decimal System arranges
            New York senators.

ἀ⋛ἀ⋛ἀ⋛ἀ⋛ἀ⋛ἀ⋛ἀ⋛ἀ⋛ἀ⋛ἀ

If Upper Manhattan began at 98.6ᵗʰ St., Harlem would also be known as the Fever-in-Fahrenheit District. If every drop of sweat dropped along a supermodel's Riverside Park jog blossomed into a trophy orchid, every drop of sweat dropped by a banker's FDR Drive jog would bloom into a diesel-dusted money-tree.

If Manhattan could be turned into a deck of Tarot cards,
    its waste disposal manager would be its Hanged Man,
        City Hall would be its Throne of Judgement,
            and Columbus Circle would be its Wheel of Fortune.

If the East Village can't be measured by acid flashbacks
    per square acre,
Chelsea can't be measured by bourbon relapses
    per brownstone,
and the Upper West Side can't be measured
    by Ritalin overdoses per rent-controlled unit.

If some New Yorkers continue to behave as if their personal microdrama has its own will-call ticket window and its own wardrobe department, the first hurricane that forms out of a Manhattan wind-tunnel will insist on being the first hurricane to sport middle, last, confirmation, pet, and pen names.

Multiply the chirps of sewer rats and crumb-pecks of pigeons by the pulse of Times Square neon to establish just one of Manhattan's metabolic rates. Divide the municipal laying-of-traps and "Don't Feed the ---" signs by the number of a particular year's Broadway dark-Mondays to establish the corrective biofeedback.

Old Manhattan sported trout streams whose denizens' scales
flashed a broad range of colors that could compete
with the prismatic splendor of its most integrated
contemporary neighborhoods.

The fakir fortune-tellers along Manhattan's most exploitative avenues who claim to know why there are so many horned animals in the standard zodiac but no winged ones should also be able to tell you why there is one white piano key for every week in a year.

Manhattan's running of the rabid squirrels could never earn a place in global culture next to Pamplona's running of the bulls because of laws of lockjaw laid down by the Treaty of Tetanus. Sometimes a mink stole's DNA dreams of resurrection and of clamping its incisors down on a Park Avenue debutante's carotid artery.

::

Certain reptiles grow successive and replaceable rows of teeth, as do certain inter-generational financial institutions. "Feed a pigeon, breed a rat" can be tweaked across species lines to "Feed a junior accounts manager, breed a hedge-fund's hubris."

In a mercifully unacted-on capitalist possibility,
a "squigeon" made from taxiderming together
a pigeon and a squirrel
could (but won't) give the Midwest's jackalope
a run for its mascot money.

The horizontal swipes of a shoe-shiner's rag forms the tim-ing-belt of the Park Avenue pedestrian engine. Ton-sensitive pressure plates sunk under a crosswalk and under a parking-space can tell us how many pounds it takes to trigger a pedestrian slow-down and how many paces it takes to outwalk a patrol car along a particular span of Park Avenue.

The glaze on a Park Avenue pavement
        can become so polished with user-mileage that
            it turns into a fun-house prism
                peering up the pant-legs of pedestrians.

<><><><><><><><><><><><><><><>

Hand-cranked smoke machines were once used to artificially accelerate the appearance of aging on building facades along Park Avenue. In a well-seasoned historical irony, many of these same buildings now house youth-reclaiming plastic surgery clinics.

Park Avenue provides proof that prostitution can be for posi-tion as well as for prey, just as pimping can be for pump-priming as well as for percentage. A séance conducted on the supper-ta-ble of an East Village injury attorney summons up the spirits of several joggers-before-jogging-had-a-name run over by several by-now-discontinued trolleys and the ghosts of several as-of-then-unnamed harassees victimized by perpetrators of crimes-to-come.

«±«±«±«±«±«±«±«±«±«±«±«±«±«±«±«±«±

On the Park Avenue Paranoia Index,
        a persecution complex becomes a persecution simplex
            when it selects a too-singular prompt
                for its feeling preyed-upon.

There are presumably thumbprint-activated helicopters waiting to flee from many of the roof-gardens of Park Avenue brownstones. Park Avenue parvenus are so used to pre-boarding planes they press ahead of pilots even on public pavements.

When Manhattanites wear their "I Voted" stickers on their sharpened elbows or on their bruised knuckles instead of over their hearts, a new chapter in Social Darwinism will have been opened. When some of our urban elite can afford to send hologram body-doubles to the office in their place, some others will send out their hologram surrogates out to perform virtual muggings.

When Werner Herzog challenged "If you're purely after facts, please buy yourself the phone directory of Manhattan," he must have known that he was using the word "buy" about one of the few things not up for sale in New York City.

∫∫∫

When our phones are able to exude scents as well as sounds and vibrations, an Olfactory Telecommunications Board will be summoned out of the broken shell of New York's Media Law Committee.

When suburban golfers aim to eventually shoot their age,
    Wall St. bankers seek to have one dollar for every sperm-cell,
        and hope to attain premium mobility
            for every cent and every seed.

:::

When cigarette burns are cut-rate tattoos on the Lower East Side, beer-can pull-rings self-assemble into costume jewelry. When the NYPD reads particular kinds of suspects in Alphabet City their rights, those rights are frequently more Mutter or Maybe than they are Miranda.

When New York City reaches peak nonchalance and peak surrealism at once, its coathangers will shrug their collective shoulders, the gloves of its sports franchises will twiddle their collective thumbs, and its concert-hall pianos will cross their collective legs.

The germs on a Lexington Avenue bordello's door-knob migrate from a janitor's hand to a senator's hand as easily as from a freelance customer advocate's hand to an interim project manager's hand because Lust is the great leveler. Since "sunshine units" are used to measure nuclear radiation, "moonshine units" should be used to locate the former Lexington Avenue speakeasies that flourished during Prohibition.

Soon, caretaker-assisted suicides all along Lexington Avenue
will begin to grow increasingly personalized and customized
and feel more like a bon-voyage departure than a
bill-past-due dropping-out
and include one's ritualistic choice in title music,
ambient fragrance, and LCD wallpaper.

‡«‡«‡«‡«‡«‡«‡«‡«‡«‡«‡«‡«‡«‡«‡

There is a subliminal code to the tying of Lexington Avenue headscarfs that spells out the history of Caribbean colonialism, with every fold and every knot signaling its own mode of resistance and degree of solidarity. As a Lexington Avenue elevator fills up, its decreasingly available territory is divided with little regard for exponential math but rather by factors of mood, aggression, and wardrobe.

78

Lexington Avenue diamond-cutters
    like Jersey-tundra oil refineries
        Crown Heights circumcision providers
        Chinatown bonsai-trimmers
            and Madison Avenue photo-retouchers
are among humanity's ways of telling our planet
that her goods aren't always good enough.

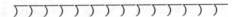

At the deep end of a Lexington Avenue secretary pool are semiotics majors and brain-trust refugees able to execute a triple-gainer from a board meeting's implied diving-board. At a Lexington Avenue charity event, bank-books clap like seals and ice-sculptures melt as slowly as the paperwork process for a West African adoptee.

If classical music played softly through a Lexington Avenue restaurant's PA indeed causes diners to order extra courses, does Mozart lead to sachertorte any more than Verdi leads to struffoli? Does Debussy lead to coq au vin any more than Stravinsky leads to sour cream-and-caviar blini?

The Chrysler Building was the tallest in the world during the span between the year that Alka Seltzer was invented and the year that the Star-Spangled Banner was officially declared the national anthem. The sum of the digits in the Empire State building's own zip code add up to the same sum as the digits in a 911 call and/or one for every character in the phrase "New York City."

Tether a too-powerful blimp to the Empire St. building
    and risk decapitating a major icon of capitalismo,
        tie a too-heavy anchor to the Staten Island Ferry,
            and risk sinking a major icon of commuterismo
                to the depths of Henry Hudson's locker.

A city of buildings supported by their skeletons instead of their skins requires more Vitamin D (for Development) than Vitamin E (for Establishment). The GE building doesn't sport a neon sign because any malfunction of its bulbs would be a self-indictment of GE's signature product.

The Flatiron Building's sharp prow
          causes cross-currents and up-drafts
                    capable of flipping a skirt into a collar
                            and a newspaper into a mask.

∞∞∞∞∞∞∞∞∞∞∞∞∞∞∞∞∞∞∞∞∞∞

The building that knows it may be slated for demolition tries to exude a raffish and haggard charm. The novel building project that knows it needs to be approved for funding tries to exude a nubile appeal.

The first 20 stories of a 100-story office building
   are merely a petty-commercial prologue
      or an artists-in-residence overture-and-undergirding
         for the uncivil offenses that occur on the uppermost floors.

Manhattan is a self-conflicted maze in which every minotaur comes with his own matador. Manhattan is an index finger moistened by the tongue of Exploration and raised to test the oncoming breeze of Novelty.

Manhattan's balance between Commerce and Politics is perhaps best "embodied" by a Macy's window-dresser smuggling social protest into her scenarios by using her mannequins as power-salute urban guerrillas.

Manhattan is a living-room set up in a reserved parking space if Brooklyn is a living-room set up inside of a moving van. Manhattan is the fumbling fugue of fingerprints that occurs whenever someone tries to place a framework around the future tense.

Manhattan is a non-kosher warning written in Cantonese
and a set of defibrillator paddles set on "Merengue"
and a Cast-Iron District crumpled into confetti
in the fist of an urban planner.

⠰⠂⠄⠰⠂⠄⠰⠂⠄⠰⠂⠄⠰⠂⠄⠰⠂⠄⠰⠂⠄⠰⠂⠄⠰⠂⠄⠰⠂⠄⠰⠂⠄⠰⠂⠄⠄

Manhattan is the produce aisle of a mini-market suffering from delusions of Amazonia and a smoke-alarm too nonchalant to be set off by a cigar stuffed into a hookah. Manhattan is the global village's over-employed town crier refusing to submit to a tongue-depressor or a tonsillectomy.

Every denizen of Manhattan standing on the Chelsea Piers would not tip the island over any more than every denizen standing on Broadway's center strip would fold it in two. Even if Broadway is merely a passing "blip" on the geologic radar, it is a still a resonating "boom" on the cultural sonar.

The statue of Garibaldi in Washington Square Park would need to be swiveled 90 degrees to face his inheritors in Little Italy and 180 degrees to face his sponsors in the Vatican. The Prometheus figure at Rockefeller Center has a bronze liver no pigeon can peck out because the Athena overlooking Herald Square has bronze eyeballs peering into the ages but incapable of detecting shoplifters.

A palm reader assigned to Manhattan's statues
      would need to be able to see a girdle of Venus in granite,
         a Mercury line in marble,
            an Apollo line in iron,
               a simian crease in steel
and all of the character traits concrete is capable of transmitting.

****
****

Wall St.'s bull statue knows to its brass bones that some tax audits are so long that they turn into mergers and some are so brief that they barely qualify as handshakes. Some Manhattan bankers must have a doppelganger statue in their cobwebbed attic that gets poorer and more virtuous and more liquidated and less tax-exempt with each passing year.

In the West Village, the Stonewall Inn and a statue of General Sheridan stare at each other from across a street, as if iconically embodying all of the Civil War tensions Manhattan's proximity to Yankee Stadium and distance from the Mason-Dixon line prevent from ever resolving.

◻◻◻◻◻◻◻◻◻◻◻◻◻◻◻◻◻◻◻◻◻◻◻◻◻◻◻◻◻◻◻

The iron eagle statue from the old Grand Central Station now being used as a lawn ornament in Secaucus knows demotion and displacement to a degree few humans ever will. The King George III that once stood in Bowling Green and was pulled down by Independence-drunk Manhattanites in 1776 was a pioneer in New York's long history of dethronements.

In a code of immobile-but-verging-on-animated
        kinetic signaling
   some of Manhattan's statues cross their arms
      or akimbo their elbows
  in a way that seems to assert
      "Permanently Refusing Any Cosmetic Repairs,"
  while some stand on tiptoe and appear to say
      "Granted Insufficient Altitude by My Genetics."

The hundreds of languages that are spoken in New York City, if placed in a Veg-O-Matic and blended, would form a mortar able to paste together the fallen Tower of Babel. Manhattan will eventually develop microdialects that append Yiddish nouns with Honduran suffixes and reroute Germanic curses with Yoruban honorifics and sweeten Croatian derogatories with Swiss uptags.

Many transitive verbs
  (like "romanticize," "idealize," "pursue," and "ogle")
    grow even more transitive in the grammatical give-and-take
      of the omnilingual New York City Transit System.

ᴑʃᴑꝾᴑʃᴑꝾᴑʃᴑꝾᴑʃᴑꝾᴑʃᴑꝾᴑʃᴑꝾᴑʃᴑ

The sign-language translator working on a mayor-elect's acceptance speech tends to use horizontally sweeping hands to replace the vertically jabbing fists of that same candidate's campaign promises.

There are certain fund-raisers in Manhattan
   where the word "finance"
      is nowhere near as important as the word "favor"
and the rhyme between the "pro" and the "quo"
   in "quid pro quo"
grows jealous of the alliteration between the
   "quid" and the "quo."

Eventually, the skid-marks on a city-dweller's
     over-swiped debit card
          spell out "overdrawn" in a digital sub-language
               only readable by the most rarefied
                    of credit-bestowing lenses.

    The bad-pun wordplay of a New York Post headline is aroused into action by cannibalism much more than by a cutting of the prime rate. Being "jaded" (in the two main senses of the word) in Chinatown comes more easily than being "stoned" (in two main senses of that word) in the Diamond District.

    If the vertical scale of the World Trade Center indeed whispered "impossible" to a trapeze artist, what uncoiling adverb does the Guggenheim ramp murmur to skateboarders and what unbudging noun does NYSE scoreboard shout at a street vendor?

If human history were Manhattan Island measured lengthwise,
     would Times Square be the medieval era
          to Chelsea's Renaissance
               and would Fort Tryon Park or Battery Park
                    be a better candidate for the End of Days?

$$\infty \approx \infty \approx \infty \approx \infty \approx \infty \approx \infty \approx \infty \approx \infty \approx \infty \approx \infty \approx \infty \approx \infty$$

    If Manhattan were a Canyon of Class-Aware Eternal Echoes, would it resound more loudly with coughs from a Randall's Island TB ward, slurps from an Art Deco oyster bar, or the whispers of a lady garment-workers' labor union forming?

Does the play-by-play announcer for a New York Knicks game
  go heavier on the exclamation marks and lighter on the ellipses
    than the announcer for a Lincoln Center ballet
      because some law of locomotion states that
        sneaker-on-hardwood
          will always require a more aggressive rhetoric
            than slipper-on-rose-petal?

<><><><><><><><><><><><><><><><>

Would a fossil menagerie made up of the names and logos
of some of New York's defunct sports franchises tell a story of
Darwinian species loss, Mendelian planned obsolescence, or
Lamarckian non-inheritance? Does Strivers' Row in Harlem
need a Slackers' Row in Alphabet City as a counter-balance and a
Spenders' Row along Fifth Avenue as a release-valve?

If Manhattan had its own mode of martial art, would its lunges
be based on its strap-hanging and its cross-blocks on its eye-rolls
and its crescent-kicks on the removal of its late February galoshes?
If every third chair at a city council meeting were a hard-wired
ejection seat, would the words "majority," "stalemate," and "tie-
breaker" all have different and more urgent meanings?

A Brooklyn-bound L-train derailment would spill as many
organic vegetables as an uptown R-train derailment would spill
tins of discount cat-food. On the A-train, some ego-driven execu-
tives are so exclusive about their personal space they seem to have
eager-to-inflate airbags installed in their elbow patches.

For reasons of asset preservation,
concert pianists stick out a foot to trick a subway door's
    electronic eye into re-opening,
        while soccer-players stick out a hand
            and mountain-climbers stick out a rump.

85

The idiom "take no quarter" takes on a new kind of sense once one is reminded that the New York City subway fare jumped directly from twenty cents to thirty cents in 1970. The eight minutes it takes solar radiation to travel from our sun to central Manhattan is a quarter of the time it takes the 7 train to travel from central Manhattan to Sunnyside.

Lenape trailblazers carved out a footpath precursor
to the D-train line
through the tulip-poplars and white pines of old Mannahatta
a gesture as uncredited as it is truly antiquarian.

The intern working for transit card swipes isn't necessarily any quicker at her errands than the intern working for tanning-bed privileges. The volunteer working for a sense of virtue isn't automatically more incorruptible than the one working for a semblance of vengeance.

Subway line 6, with a stop named for a millionaire trader in beaver pelts and a stop named for the patron saint of the poor and needy, is silently reveling in its own brand of inter-platform historical irony.

Carnegie Hall: an auditorium named for a steel magnate with some of the best acoustics in the world for the steel-wire strings of a grand piano. Bryant Park: a greensward named for a pagan-leaning Romantic poet and taken over by a pagan-denying Christmas Village every autumn.

Did the number of fedoras, pork pies, and straw boaters
that showed up for Thelonious Monk's funeral
at St. Peter's Church
rival the number of shaven heads and vertically painted
forehead lines
that show up for the average Buddhist monk's?

The oboe section of the New York Philharmonic can resemble a small field of fledgling Viennese maples swaying during certain moments of a Mozart concerto and small outfit of howitzers standing erect during the peak-fever mom ents of a Wagner opera.

When Miles Davis turned his back on a Village Vanguard
    audience during a trumpet solo,
he could seem to be facing a spot somewhere between
    Mecca and Andalusia
but was actually facing some point of pilgrimage
    in between St. Louis and Kansas City.

::

A vinyl record of a Duke Ellington suite slowed to five revolutions-per-minute tolls a bell for every fit of melancholy ever suffered in Manhattan — that same record sped up by a factor of ten sounds likes its grooves are about to jump their tracks like an unmanned A-train.

Manhattan's broomhandle-and-bucket drum corps are a semaphore system signaling across the city's most taciturn barricades at moments of peak commuter exhaustion, blasting holes in the city's most blasé facades with an arsenal of paradiddles and ratamacues.

If the game of Monopoly were based on a caricature of 1970s Manhattan instead of an idealized Atlantic City, the pewter Scottish terrier would be replaced with a steel-trap attack Doberman and the pewter thimble would be replaced with brass knuckles.

If New York City's upper classes put the phonetic "Oz"
    in the word "cosmopolis,"
        its working classes provided the "mop"
            and its earliest philosophers questioned its "is."

If a Manhattan office building were a totem-pole, its scavenging ravens and coyotes and predatory owls would radically outnumber its preyed-upon salmons and woodpeckers. If Manhattan had its own version of the Magna Carta, it would by now have more footnotes than a tax-code overhaul and more amendments than a forced confession.

If New Yorkers had some voluntary say or input into where they were conceived by their parents, the secure confines of a Plaza Hotel penthouse would only presumably outrank a leaky rowboat on the Central Park reservoir.

>d>d>d>d>d>d>d>d>d>d>d>d>d>d>d>d>d>d>d>

If the prices of a subway ride and a pizza-slice do tend to correlate, the price of a cab-ride and a net-packed salami should learn to pace warily around one another. If the term "Big Apple" was in fact invented by New Orleans race-track stable-hands, the Crescent City is owed a "Big Okra" by the stable-hands of Aqueduct and Belmont Park.

If the buried plague victims under Washington Square Park begin seeping their thawing viruses upward, insurance policies will scramble to issue a few new provisos while city planners scramble to provide some sense of interception.

The heavy braces that prevent Manhattan's bridges from swaying are shaped like vowels (particularly U-clamps or O-sleeves) more often than consonants, even though vowels and not consonants most often allow our spoken words to sway.

Hart Crane heard a resonating harp in the steel suspension cables
    of the Brooklyn Bridge
without ever noticing the Stratocaster-to-be
    in the Williamsburg Bridge,
the bagpipes skirling out of the bracings of the Hell Gate,
or the Alpine horns blown by northerly winds
    all along the Spuyten Duyvil.

#############################

A bridge named for George Washington connects a Jersey borough that still calls itself a "fort" and the Manhattan neighborhood that tastes most supremely of the Caribbean. A tunnel named for Abraham Lincoln connects the Jersey town where our first secretary of the treasury was killed and that portion of midtown trying to erase any residue of Hell's Kitchen with the scouring-pad of gentrification.

The very notion of a "speed limit" is as remote and redundant
    in bumper-to-bumper Brooklyn Bridge taxi traffic
        as it is an idle threat and an irrelevance
            on the open acreage of Bonneville's Salt Flats.

∫∫∫

For the George Washington Bridge or the Lincoln Tunnel to lead directly out onto the FDR Drive or Kennedy Airport would require several geologic impeachments, cartographic re-elections, and spatial campaign swindles.

Suicide leaps from all nineteen of Manhattan's bridges combined cannot keep pace with the Golden Gate Bridge, despite the Bay Area's soul-healing New Age pretenses and New York's off-handed claims of nihistic expertise.

A Manhattan entrance-poll can't afford any appearance of interrogation unless an impending exit-poll promises to avoid the taint of Inquisition and any and all electioneering agrees to aim for indifference.

New York's overcrowded graveyards will eventually have to bury their clients on a more vertical or virtual plan, with headstones that roll names like stops on a tour-bus's marquee and caskets that revolve like a department-store door.

::

Manhattan should be saddled with a half-century handicap when competing against Cleveland and Detroit for Endangered Capital of the Second American Century and granted a cultural-capital infusion when competing with London and Beijing for Capital of the New Millennium.

In a 90-second history of Manhattan,
    WW1 is a five-second drumroll on a military snare
        Prohibition is a drumming of figures on a windowpane
      The Great Depression is a clapping of chapped hands
and the 1950's are a cymbal-crash at a Catskills resort.

Virginia has its Civil War re-enactors, its Pentagon recipients, and its would-be Mason-Dixon straddlers; Manhattan has its Black Friday re-enactors, its U.N. incipients, and its would-be Park Avenue straddlers. More so than the criminally insane, Manhattan suffers from the criminally indifferent, the criminally indistinguishable, the criminally indirect, and the criminally inconspicuous.

A north-to-south tongue depressor shaped like Manhattan Island
would leave a Battery Tunnel-shaped impression
    on a patient's tip-most taste-buds
    and a Marble Hill-shaped impression near its gag-reflex.

A few intuitive laws of Manhattan require that the number of
horizontal slats on a park bench have a direct relation to the species of loiterer it attracts. The geometric laws of Manhattan aren't
bothered by West 4th St. crossing West 10th St., causing Descartes
and Euclid to tremble in their respective graves.

The mathematically ironic laws of Manhattan dictated that
the 110 floors of the former Twin Towers featured 110 volts com-
ing out of their wall-plugs to commemorate 110th St. as Harlem's
lower gateway.

□□□□□□□□□□□□□□□□□□□□□□□□□□□□□□□□□□

The prosthetic laws of Manhattan state that what was stored
behind Kurt Russell's eye-patch in *Escape from New York* is a rival
for what was stored inside of Peter Stuyvesant's wooden leg during
Settlement of New Amsterdam.

The structural laws of Manhattan observe
    that the more-provisional skating rink at Bryant Park
        seems to inspire fewer triple-axels and camel-spins
            than the more-august skating rink
                at Rockefeller Center.

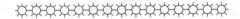

The weaponized laws of Manhattan know that those U.S.
Coast Guards who patrol New York Harbor gripping swiv-
el-mounted 240 Bravo machine-guns all day long are on Oceanic,
Urban, and Ego alert all at once.

The spiritual laws of Manhattan take scant note that the iron curlicue latticework of St. Patrick's Cathedral looks like a tribute to the very serpents that St. Patrick slew. The memorial laws of Manhattan remember that the picket lines protesting the demolition of the original Penn Station were as serpentine as a peace march, as agitated as a drum-circle turning into a mosh-pit, and as wobbly as a pulled pushcart.

In some alternate dimension of melodic parallelism, "Harlem Nocturne" played at noon shares a turnaround chord with "Chelsea Morning" played at sunset. In a dimension of scalar justice, high-rise buildings that sport progressively higher ceilings on their progressively higher floors resemble an accordion playing a major-key Charlie Parker solo.

A New York City radiator turning on,
    with all of its pings, knocks, and wheezes,
        can sound like a pointillist parody of a Brahms overture
           arguing with a mid-period John Cage piece based
              on I-Ching patterns.

⁘⁝⁘⁝⁘⁝⁘⁝⁘⁝⁘⁝⁘⁝⁘⁝⁘⁝⁘⁝⁘⁝⁘

That person recorded laughing at the wrong moments on a Lenny Bruce bootleg or applauding during an off-moment in a John Coltrane solo was more likely to grow up to be a Manhattan comptroller than a gallery curator.

In surrealistically post-American Manhattan,
    the original sheet music to Gershwin's "Rhapsody in Blue"
        refuses to be torn into absorbent confetti
           to line the cage of the American Eagle.

A violin with strings made from ratgut instead of catgut,
    when playing a Mozart adagio,
        would be zoologically truer to Yorktown in Manhattan
        and artistically less true to
            New York's half-sister city of Vienna at once.

In an alternate dimension more attentive to ores and alloys,
the metal detector leading into a Madison Square Garden concert
squeals on faux-silver and bellows at body-piercings and groans at
gold-plating.

Even if hemmed in by urban jungle at every angle, a June wedding catered by an East Village organic-food co-op will be heavy
on the can't-be-canned carbohydrates and scanty on the predator
proteins.

If Flouting can indeed be a matter of Flaunting,
    East Village parking-ticket scofflaws
        wallpaper their tenements with warrants
            in a different pattern of layering
            than freelance writers wallpaper their walk-ups
                with rejection slips.

                ꝹꝹꝹꝹꝹꝹꝹꝹꝹꝹꝹꝹꝹꝹꝹꝹꝹꝹꝹꝹꝹꝹꝹ

Some East Village potholes, boarded windows,
    and graffiti'd mailboxes
        have endured for so long and intensified
            into such familiarity
they can practically file for protected landmark status.

Many of the asymmetrical haircuts that pervaded the 1980's
East Village were so languidly lopsided they leaned toward "tipping-point" and away from "tonsorial" as much as they leaned toward
"tumultuous" and away from "tiered."

For many an East Village restauranteur, arrogantly risking that an eatery's Michelin star will implode in a premature supernova also insures that it won't be asked to join a neighborhood constellation and will be able to skip the white-dwarf stage of a Sunday buffet.

That vacant space in many an East Villager's wallet that would have been occupied by a driver's-license (in a less pedestrian town) tends to house either an esoterically snobbish proof-of-membership card or a deliriously democratic discount-coupon.

When the children of stockbrokers build sandcastles flattering the World Trade Center on Jones Beach, children of home care providers build sandcastles satirizing the U.N. Building on Far Rockaway.

When essence-of-Manhattan comes in a squeeze-bottle,
    ambience-of-Brooklyn will come in a re-sealable packet
        and aura-of-Bronx in a pop-top tallboy.

ﬞﾛﾑﾛﾛﾛﾛﾛﾛﾛﾛﾛﾛﾛ

When recess at an Upper East Side prep academy gets prolonged by a debate over blue- chip stocks or St. Tropez getaways, Wall St.'s shark tank has overflowed its generational confines. When loans are so predatory they have fangs for fine print, Hangman's Elm in Washington Square Park begins to swing its subliminal noose in a certain kind of insurgent breeze.

When a UN teleprompter moonlights as a karaoke teleprompter
    it is showing an Eastern-hemisphere bias
        and a willingness to be baptized in spilled soju
            and sake alike.

When a performance space turns into a franchise pharmacy, Manhattan's self-cannibalism cuts another notch on its own fangs and goes looking for a public housing tower to convert into a missile silo.

When, in the refracting mirror of battle-readiness,
municipal police hide their badge numbers behind masking tape,
protestors wrap their heads in duct-taped Styrofoam
and news outlets wrap their boom-mikes in cellophane.

If the half-emptied drinks at a midtown fundraiser are question marks, the half-full drinks at a Bowery dive are exclamation-points-in-the-making. As mid-town brunches inch closer to lunch and further away from breakfast, their options become more open-ended and less orange-driven and more option-heavy and less egg–centered.

For reasons of environment-influencing-outcome
fortune-cookies can tend toward the oracular on Orchard St.,
the God-contesting on Grand Avenue,
and the metaphysically speculative on Mott St.

Ж Ж Ж Ж Ж Ж Ж Ж Ж Ж Ж Ж Ж

It is easier to boil beans on the top floor of the Freedom Tower and easier to cure pork in the deepest unused tunnel of the MTA because the polar impulses of urban Aspiration and Excavation shared a common drive toward Expediting.

As a general principle of Washington Heights counter-balance,
the more weary the sprawl of a bodega's overfed cat,
the more piquant its coffee
and the more longshot a bodega's lottery tickets,
the more dependable its dry goods.

Gramercy Park assisted-living dictum: since a cardiac episode is often accompanied by the smell of burning toast, a make-believe migraine should be accompanied by the smell of frozen waffle and a feigned arthritis by the smell of French-toast batter.

If comic-book captions are correct and the muzzle-flash from a pistol-barrel emits a four-letter "bang," what word does the crackle of a coal-burning pizza oven or the bubbling of a bagel-vat spell out in the funny-paper confines of New York City food prep?

Battery Park's endangered species list includes the unavoided bill collector and the unanticipated organ donor. Only a few Battery Parkers are nostalgic for a time when our semi-taskers and pseudo-taskers outnumbered our multi-taskers and our Type Z personalities could roll their eyes at our conferencing-while-jogging Type A personalities.

A straw fedora's iridescent headband-plumage
    is an affront to the most insecure of Battery Park pigeons
        an oil-spill to the most ecologically-minded of
           Red Hook pigeons
               and an endgoal for the most aspirational of
               Park Avenue pigeons.

A Battery Park ballerina's bunions, blisters, and bruises all believe in building one's bastion out of self-brutalizing. Less masochistically, little is as intense and yet as unspoken as a Battery Park fixed-gear bike's gratitude that Manhattan is no longer the "hilly island" described by the Lenape and the Mohican.

"Like a character in a novel who doesn't know he's speaking prose inside of quotation marks, some Battery Park bankers don't realize they're speaking half-remembered statistics over lunch and pending annuities in their sleep."

Because New Yorkers balance so delicately between Detachment and Invasiveness, there is an eager-to-convene appeals court sitting on practically every bench in Battery Park and a little-assembly-required probate-panel at nearly every outdoor chessboard.

Battery Park's future heart-surgeon cabbies seem to take corners as recklessly as its ex-KGB cabbies do because cab-life intensifies primeval urgencies with no respect for former or eventual status.

If Manhattan were indeed sold for beads by a native tribe in some alternative dimension of unhistoric hyperbole, Queens was swapped for a set of sequins, the Bronx was traded for a box of sharkskin suits, and Staten Island was gotten for a Neapolitan pizza recipe.

If Wall St. ever begins to classify its "dead-cat bounces"
    more specifically,
        it will begin suffering "Siamese slumps,"
           "calico caroms," "tabby trajectories," and
              "marmalade meltdowns" as well.

«±«±«±«±«±«±«±«±«±«±«±«±«±«±«±«±«±

If the ice cubes in a rye cocktail could tinkle out ragtime jazz or Chopin minuets in one part of town, the ice cubes in a carafe of mango-loaded sangria could tinkle out merengue or compas in another, all in the name of Animism Equity. If the Velázquez oil portraits and the Rose Period Picassos begin arguing over the Spanish Civil War, you have entered a museum with too historicist a mind-frame.

If Judgment Day agrees to begin its proceedings in Manhattan,
the collective bribe offered for its postponement
would include Wall St.'s Caribbean war chest,
the U.N.'s Esperanto fund, and
Madison Avenue's self-minted media currency.

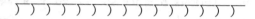

If Hercule's ordeals were updated in Lower Manhattan, his twelve labors would include retuning the earphones at Electric Lady studios to the Hudson's tidal hiss, bisecting alternate-side-of-the-street-parking during a ticker-tape blizzard, making napalm out of papaya froth, and building a side-loading fragmentation device out of a St. Mark's Place hookah.

If Brooklyn's Park Slope grows any more slanted, its gentrification will slide into one of Manhattan's own predatorial maws like an after-dynasty mint.

The remote control to a 292-inch flat-screen in Soho dreams about rearranging the flight patterns of Piper Cubs preparing for touch-down into Newark. The hi-res micro-camera implanted on a Soho home-care provider's lapel is witness to innumerable acts of luxury-based-larceny and larceny-based luxury.

Blindfold a Soho lawyer and spin him on a turntable
and you'll end up with a class-action suit
pinned to the tail of a Riverside Park picnic
or a formal grievance flung out
in the general direction of a charity ball.

One can overhear a large library's worth of words spoken in Soho's streets every day, but some blocks are more plumber's manual than romance-novel and some are more forbidden scripture than social registry.

Only one out of five Soho orthodontists who
    maintain a trophy mistress in a hunting cabin
        or on a fishing boat
    actually believes in post-Darwinian natural de-selection,
    inherited characteristics able to leap a
        prep-school enrollment lottery,
          or survival-of-the-most-scholarshipped.

✧✧✧✧✧✧✧✧✧✧✧✧✧✧✧

Soho's four surviving cobblestone streets laid end to end could be renamed the Horseless Carriage Half-Mile, El Champs Cord du Roy, or Old New Amsterdam Avenue. These same cobblestone streets rearranged into the spiral hourglass of a DNA helix would serve as the commemorative chromosomes of Manhattan's colonial genome.

The ceiling fans in a Soho hotel lobby devoted to a classical Roman motif spin calendar-wise as well as clockwise just as surely as the windshield wipers of a Soho limousine swing from urgent-to-impatient as well as side-to-side.

New Yorkers know that the devil is in the derailings and deafenings and disbarments as well as in the details. Bend a New York Post headline into wraparound form so it resembles a ring of Saturn and its scandals turn stellar and gossip turns galactic.

Prior to its counter-clockwise continental drift,
New York was as geologically attached to North Africa
as it is now emotionally attached to sudden trends
in Moroccan silk and Liberian coffee,
upticks in the Nigerian petrol market
and downturns in Tanzanian gold-mining.

Some New York job titles are followed by so many abbreviations they dissolve into a status soup, while some are prefixed by so many titles they congeal into a crème-brulee crust. The "M" in "Manhattan" is the "w" in "New York" in mid-cartwheel only where the double "t"'s are impromptu grave-markers and the "a"'s are gasps of relief.

The oversized Camel billboard that used to blow cough-inducing smoke rings as big across as hula hoops was New York's largest-ever affront to the pristine whiteness of the surgeon general's naval uniform.

The collective biomass of Manhattan
contains more microbe than man,
more virus than visitor,
more cyanobacteria than citizen,
and more nematode than native New Yorker.

Counter-intuitively, the man who boldly "purchased" Manhattan, Peter Minuit, sported a moniker resembling the name of a dance of tentative, mincing steps. Anti-intuitively, the mayor who oversaw Manhattan's nearest brush with bankrupcty, Abe Beame, sported a surname homophonic with a support-structure for a stable edifice.

Sometimes our collective urban behavior tells us that we are still adjusting to our having evolved into mammal-hood and still uneasy at having evolved away from single-celled microbe-hood. Sometimes a Mt. Sinai cancer patient heals more rapidly if his window pretends to look out on a gentleman's club or an off-track betting parlor rather than on a willow tree or a winding stream, because Vice can be a vitalizing force.

Sometimes a downtown coffee house's furniture is so increasingly mismatched it slowly dwindles from "eclectic" to "uncoordinated" to "accidental." Sometimes the small metal flag that controlled a pre-digital taxi's meter refused to be saluted because the checker-board of a yellow cab was an emblem of economic and automotive mobility. Sometimes the umlauts and diagonally crossed vowels in a cabbie's surname refuse to disappear because taxi-driving is a key component in Manhattan's avenue-climbing Esperanto.

****
****

Sometimes the security deposit on a Thompson St. apartment spends its interest-earning interim sunning itself on a deck-chair in St. Thomas. Sometimes an apartment's asking price gets answered half in the affirmative and half in the interrogative and blurs the line between decimals and ellipses.

Sometimes the only antidote to an Avenue A irony epidemic
   is a forced immigration of excessive earnestness
     that is every bit as encumbered and ungainly
      as the ailment it addresses.

Sometimes a Manhattan microbrewery is so micro- its molecules are weapons-grade mutation materials bent on dissolving the boundaries between beer, ale, and stout. Sometimes the thought-bubble above a drunken city comptroller's head is a thunder-cloud, even when the speech-bubble emerging from his mouth is a trial balloon.

Sometimes the fountain at Lincoln Center seem to spume and billow when infuriated by certain goings-on with the Dow Jones Industrial Average, and the fountain at Washington Square seems set off by upticks in the price of organic tofu.

The mayor of New York doesn't get access to nuclear launch codes because night-club bouncers don't get access to weapons-grade trampolines, and the mayor doesn't use oyster-shell necklaces to purchase landfill space because bouncers don't use the Domesday Book to determine entrance-levels.

Ed Koch once characterized New York life as a battle between
    "the knife of corruption" and "the scalpel of the law"
        without mentioning the brass-knuckles of bravado,
            the sand-bag of slander,
                and the gravity-knife of graft
                    that also reside in the urban armory.

****
****

Since a mayor is sworn in on a Bible, a district attorney should be sworn in on a gossip column, a comptroller on a half-balanced ledger, a judicial delegate on a torn ballet, and a council member on a brown-bag lunch order.

Mayor LaGuardia preferred to be referred to by his Air Force rank, "Major," but river-laced New York City has never elected a mayor deserving of "Rear Admiral" or "Commodore" despite the occasional castaway, freebooter, kayaker and buccaneer.

A New York City mayor knows that a cynic's perspective
    is no less blurry than an idealist's,
        but is blurred with premature dismissals
        instead of premature acceptances.

Since Mayor LaGuardia was willing to read the Sunday comics over the radio, Mayor Walker should have read edited-out pages from *The Great Gatsby*, Mayor Lindsay should have read bootlegged passages from Ian Fleming novels without security clearance, and Mayor Koch should have read from the portions of his own unpublished film criticism that addressed urban angst in the post-*Godfather* era.

The beheaded broom-handles used to play Alphabet City stickball are only occasionally "recapitated" for more domestic chores. Certain actions undertaken in Alphabet City have an At Your Own Risk proviso sewn into their inseam, bordered by upside-down and rightside-up exclamation points at either end.

If the East River is Alphabet City's missing Avenue E,
    the heaving Hudson River can be accused of putting
        the H in Hell's Kitchen
            and the Harlem River can be credited
                with rolling the "r" in Marble Hill.

:✻:✻:✻:✻:✻:✻:✻:✻:✻:✻:✻:✻::✻:✻:✻:

In Alphabet City's tenement hallways, ammonia sterilizes mildew and bacteria into an agonized and writhing molecular frenzy that would look cruel and sadistic to a species-neutral perspective. In some parallel dimension, there is a burglar alarm in an alternative Alphabet City that imitates one of Bob Dylan's 1964 harmonica solos at peak protest-wheeze.

Censored Alphabet City daydreams: convicted junk-bond traders being fed to library lions in Yankee Stadium, Earth Day and Arbor Day being placed in the victory column for Tompkins Square and in the loss column for Wall St., and Avenue A liquor-lockers with combinations taken from old Irish Sweepstakes lottery tickets.

❋:❋:❋:❋:❋:❋:❋:❋:❋:❋:❋:❋:❋:❋:❋

A too-hasty "crash" course in speaking Alphabet City Manhattanese will indeed bend your phonetic fender and put a crimp in your grammatical gas tank. The hominid fossil record shows our former gill structures developing into our current ears, and indeed listening to Alphabet City gossip is often like swimming though riptides of rumor.

New York's mayors have chronically suffered from History's lint-trap not being able to separate rancor from rumor nor scandal from suspense. If every mayor in New York history were memorialized in bobble-head doll form, some would have a special lateral gear for crucial moments of indecision.

If *Forbes* had an Infernal 5,000 to offset its Top 500, no business with a roll-down gate to guard its plate-glass window would qualify for either. If the most regretted tattoo in Tribeca looks more like a mutual bond than a tuxedo's reversible lining, the most regretted tattoo in Gramercy Park looks more like an eviction notice than a mislaid manhole cover.

If the Plaza Hotel redecorated by Groucho Marx would resemble a class-warfare coliseum, it would resemble a Tuscan cottage invaded by tumbleweeds if redecorated by Chico, and a music hall whose fiddles have been sawed in two by its termites if redecorated by Harpo.

If the orange of a New York Knick uniform is trying to homeo-pathically influence the orange of a regulation basketball hoop's metal rim, the white of a New York Ranger uniform is trying to perform an act of magic on the white of a hockey-goal's net. If some national anthems require an open hand placed over one's heart, some of New York's neighborhood anthems require closed fists pounding on one's own kneecaps.

If subway delays are measured in Manhattan minutes,
    ferry cancelations are measured in Staten Island split-seconds
      and taxi-meter malfunctions in Newark nano-dots.

If a nuclear treaty between New York City and Newark ever becomes necessary, it would need to be about megaton mergers as well as inter-city arms-effacement. If a pre-nuptial agreement between Manhattan and Jersey City is ever ventured, it will need to measure its alimony allotment in acreage and its spinoff-support in subway lines.

If three Central Parks' worth of trees are indeed needed to print the *Sunday New York Times*, perhaps Japanese maples would best suit the Asia Pacific pages, horse-chestnuts best serve the racing column, and Trees of Heaven best supply the obituaries...

The posterior prints laid down by Columbia University's most recent sit-down strike are the punctuation marks of protest. A certain kind of historically ultra-absorbent pavement can fossilize a disgruntled college sophomore's spittle for posterity.

There are rain-spattered moments
near Cooper Union's painting studios
when Manhattan looks like a half-erased Matisse
and a half-finished Rembrandt
even as its pedestrians resist resembling
a Duchamp readymade at their most off-the-rack
or a Calder mobile at their most hectically kinetic.

****
****

If academic justice took aspiration into account, an especially long-winded King's College commencement address would be forced to pay a carbon dioxide emission-tax to maintain the vows of silence at a nearby monastery.

For career-fearing college seniors,
a mid-morning matinee used to be Manhattan medicine
for a certain kind of Monday malaise
but has since been trumped by
diversions more dependent on the techtopian
than the ticket-booth.

ᴑꙄᴑʃᴑꙄᴑʃᴑꙄᴑʃᴑꙄᴑʃᴑꙄᴑʃᴑᴑʃᴑꙄᴑ

The eraser dust in a Lower East Side parochial school is no more likely to reassemble into a Biblical quote on teacher-reverence than the eraser dust at an uptown charter school is to reassemble into a public safety warning on class peril.

A brief index of yet-undiagnosed Manhattan ailments:
Columbia Admissions Exam Brain Fluke,
Times Square Retina Burn,
Park Bench Waffle-Back Osmosis,
Avenue F Delusional Placement Syndrome,
Comedy Club Canned-Laughter Botulism.

The blue of a Manhattan sky is enhanced and underwritten by the blue-plate specials along its Geriatric Row and blue-vein specials in its cosmetic surgery clinics and blue-stocking specials among Chelsea's spinster confederation and blue-law specials in the NYPD's most esoteric inner circles.

Dances invented but never popularized in Manhattan:
  the Tammany Hall Tuxedo Tan-line,
    the Half-Renewed Wedding Vow Waltz,
      the Birdland Binocular-Mimic, the Roseland Petal-Strew,
        and the More Papaya than Pineapple Fruit-Salad Headdress.

:✳:✳:✳:✳:✳:✳:✳:✳:✳:✳:✳:✳:✳:✳:

Stellar Sour Grapes: the evening stars that Manhattan's halogen and neon render invisible are largely extinct, imploded relics anyway, supernova'd long before the astral-urban explosion of the Great White Way and the pulsar field of a Times Square toteboard.

Much of Manhattan's real estate is sold not "as is" but
  "as was" (in the case of vintage brownstones)
    or "as will be" (in the case of vacant lots)
      or "as if" (in the case of airspace).

Ж Ж Ж Ж Ж Ж Ж Ж Ж Ж Ж Ж Ж

The native American Elms of Manhattan fought off Dutch Elm Disease in a struggle that mirrored an earlier, human conflict on the island. The Star Magnolias, Sugar Maples, and Flowering Dogwoods of Central Park likewise raise their own branches in testimony to the city's host of aboriginal crimes.

Now that Manhattan's newsrooms are no longer filled with cigar-smoke, they must seek new ways to maintain their enigmatic and oracular sense of Haze. Now that Manhattan's former speakeasys no longer have any need for silence, they must seek new ways to maintain their obscure sense of Selectivity.

Classism Parable:

A tour-bus's "Not in Service" sign spelled out in lights is still itself on-duty from the perspective of a bulb or a fuse.

Narcissism Parable:

New York City runs on its own specially customized and non-standard version of Eastern Standard Time that speeds up during commercial breaks and slows down during self-references.

Elitism Parable:

"I'm with the Nobel Laureate" T-shirts would sell considerably better in Manhattan than anywhere else on the planet, even when adjusting for an immigration surcharge.

※ ※ ※ ※ ※ ※ ※ ※ ※ ※ ※

Relativism Parable:

The Wall St. Riviera, the Morningside West Bank, and the FDR Ivory Coast all have different takes on what it means to be "waterfront."

Animism Parable:

If Jackson Pollock's *Lavender Mist* jumped off the canvas and came to life, it would throw a few of its loops and lassos around the necks of a few gallery curators.

Separatism Parable:

Seating-sections at Carnegie Hall aren't yet segregated into lounger, deck, rocking, and wicker because Radio City Music Hall doesn't contain an ergonomics embassy.

Absolutism Parable:

The star that represents the state of New York on the American flag doesn't have a precise location, but it surely must occupy something close to a corner or a center if justice be done.

Stoicism Parable:

The last Chico Marx accent on Mulberry St. is being kept alive on a pump-driven dialect resuscitator wired directly to the big-toe pulse of Italy's boot.

There comes a time in a Manhattan career criminal's old age when his "prior" arrests can be seen from their posterior side. There are several million less shadows in Manhattan since we replaced our gas lamps with neon and halogen, but just as many shadow-haunted stories of urban horror as ever before.

Fortunately even Manhattanite "character armor"
    has a flip-up visor,
        a convertible breastplate,
            and a self-administered oil-can
                that can relieve its isolation from time to time.

∫∫∫

The glacier that sliced Long Island from the mainland didn't expect residuals or royalties from the snoboisie of Manhattan any more than the tectonic flux that lifted Morningside Heights to its current altitude expected an honorary doctorate from Columbia's school of engineering.

Gurgling-water ringtones are ineffective
    too near Central Park's Bethesda Fountain
        because vibrating alerts are ineffective
            while riding Coney Island's Cyclone
                and a dial-up modem message alert
                    cannot be heard by a pre-Edison ear-horn.

Mercifully, the moon over Manhattan is more frequently in "nonchalant side-glance" or "eyebrows arched ironically" mode than in "pitiless gaze" mode. Less charitably, the noonday August sun over Manhattan sports a glare that sends pedestrians scurrying along avenues like pellets of sweat along half-clad limbs.

Method-acting was largely developed in Manhattan, but New York's workaday histrionics also involve method-shopping, method-biking, and method-drinking—all which require stunt-doubling for one's self and keeping in character even at the cost of personal calamity.

The eventual "Ellis" Island being called Gull Island by its original Indian inhabitants and Oyster Island by its succeeding Dutch inhabitants says something about the respective mindsets of aboriginals and colonialists and the spirit-uses of water-fowl and mollusks. On Ellis Island, would-be immigrants suspected of insanity had a chalk "X" written on their coats that claimed (clinically if not convincingly) not to stand for "Xenophobia." Ellis Island closed just as more and more incomers began checking the spaces in between boxes on immigration forms, as the idea of "identity" began requiring more and more asterisks and endnotes.

The narrowing of the Hudson River has led to
    a faster current, a deeper channel, and more scoured river-bottom,
        sending silt and sediment out into the ocean
            as fast as an investment bank offloads its mishaps
          onto its non-investors.

The Titanic was scheduled to arrive in New York Harbor during a full lunar eclipse, as if to karmically overcompensate for the first European galleon to ever enter said harbor being named the Half Moon.

Fifth Avenue is Manhattan's Great Divide,
    a commerce-driven center border that separates
        the spuming headwaters of the East Side
            from the tumbling undercurrents of the West Side.

«±«±«±«±«±«±«±«±«±«±«±«±«±«±«±«±«±«

Minetta Creek is one of Manhattan's phantom waterways, supposedly snuffed out with landfill long ago but reportedly still rising out of people's drainpipes, air-vents and basement floorboards at inconvenient moments. This creek stands (and flows) as a half-hidden metaphor for much of the city's other forms of denial and repression.

A semi-urban legend claims that a single pillar holds Manhattan above its surrounding waters, but no version of this legend yet claims said pillar will one day rotate the island like a Studio 54 special mix played at 45 spins per minute during a disco-themed Doomsday reckoning.

In a parallel universe's bookkeeping, all of the misfiled items in the New York Public library constitute a vagrant and elusive literary genre all their own. In a parallel-universe midtown, that brief moment when the traffic lights at 42nd and Eighth show red in all four directions is a Pedestrian's Purgatory and a Limo-Driver's Limbo at once.

In a parallel-universe Manhattan where letters amalgamate like zip-codes, Spanish Enclave Told To Latinize Edgecombe (SETTLE) and Quadrangle Under Astor Square Allowing Roadwork (QUASAR), are both acronyms waiting to join the borough's alphabet soup.

∫∫∫

In a parallel-universe Lincoln Center, the horned helmets at a Wagnerian opera can point backward to the Black Forest and ahead to Valhalla at the same time. In a parallel-universe art auction, the platinum of Andy Warhol's wig-collection could bankrupt Fort Knox if it wanted to.

In a parallel-universe political arrangement,
     the ghosts who haunt Gracie Mansion
          know how to eat unnoticed from multinational buffets,
               rewind footprints from a Persian carpet,
                 and erase incoming messages
                     from a paranormal investigator's
                     answering service.

::

In a parallel-universe Manhattan mediasphere, there are lost episodes of *The Honeymooners* so lost that they are orbiting above the ozone layer looking for a docking station. In a parallel-universe Manhattan dreamscape, King Kong would have climbed the Riverside Church steeple and swatted away biplanes until our nation's gold standard had been replaced by a Carnegie Deli condiment standard.

In a parallel dimension of acoustic omen, there is an air-raid siren in the belfry of St. Paul's Cathedral that has been apocalyptically agnostic ever since the overlap between the Second Vatican Council and Beatlemania.

The dividing line running down the center of 14th Street near Union Square is occasionally turned into accidental Morse code by a chipping or fading of its paint, spelling out accidental oracles for the chariots of the urban gods. If the reunification of the East and West Villages comes at the expense of existential diversity, the separation of North Union Square from South Union Square is a splitting of subcultural hairs.

Union Square loiterers know
    that sometimes it takes an axe made out of Whatever
        to cut down a tree made out of Regardless
        and a backbone made of Nonchalant
            to lay comfortably on a lawn made of No Loitering.

.·.·.·.·.·.·.·.·.·.·.·.·.·.·.·.·.·.·.·.

Some tourists calmly manage a secular pilgrimage to St. Patrick's Cathedral, an economic safari to Wall St., and a hallucinogenic vision-quest to Union Square in a single day. A pension-fund manager on lunch break understandably threads through a Union Square crowd as if being pursued by torch-bearing retirees.

Because currency-transfer has very definite limits
    the ATM's on Union Square cannot spit out bus tickets
        to Union City
    any more than the ATM's in the UN can dispense itineraries
        to Red Square
    or the ATM's near Columbus Circle
        emit Camp Hiawatha brochures.

The fish-eye lens installed in the peephole of a Union Square dietician clinic's front door distorts a Modigliani anorexic into a Rubens obesity and an El Greco ectomorph into a Henry Moore fireplug.

There is a precise autumnal moment when the gold of Union Square oak-leaves, and the yellow of district-court legal memo-pads, and the russet of bare Riverside Park twigs and Brown University applications are all within rustling distance of one another.

On the Upper West Side, the "roar" of the Roaring 1920's was depressed into a murmur by the 1930's, fanned into a war-cry by the 1940's, flattened into a dial-tone by the 1950's and raised into a mantra by the 1960's.

Not knowing someone "from Adam"
    and not knowing them from Absalom, Ahab, or Abraham
        are matters of intimacy, urgency and impressiveness
            on the Upper West Side.

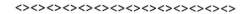

An Upper West Side ballerina's stalker hides behind lamp-posts where an opera-singer's stalker hides behind food-carts for reasons of latitude as well as body-contour. Someday, more militantly protective Upper West Side intercoms will be able to translate, buffer, commodify, and monetize messages en route from a lobby to a penthouse.

An organ-harvesting underground along the Upper West Side
    would be a network of paid-off pancreases and
        loan-lease livers and collateral kidneys
            all nostalgic for the previous incarnations
        and novel to their new owners.

The mothballs in an Upper West Side matron's cedar closet are the fixed stars to her Russian sable coat's dark matter and the frozen electrons scattered around the nucleus of her chinchilla stole. A year of daily X-rays at an Upper West Side clinic might well make said matron glow like a herd of neon plankton floating off Far Rockaway given an inelegant enough level of exposure.

In terms of honorific accoutrements, the more likely an Upper West Side deli butcher is to call you "boss," the more likely he is to slice thick. The more likely a barmaid is to call you "tiger," the more likely she is to double-dose. The more likely shoeshine buffers are to call you "chief," the more likely they are to bring your wingtips to a mirror gleam.

As we normalize our relations with Cuba in the form of cancelled embargos, we need to stop abnormalizing our relations with Wall St. in the form of casino welfare. World Wars 2.1 and 2.2 have already been waged and won by Wall St.'s supercomputers in some deep-storage version of Manifest Destiny .

Wall St. seems to insist that the "-ize" in
    "amortize," "securitize," "annuitize," and "collateralize"
        is the same one found in "prize"
            despite its preference for "bonus" over "award"
                and its favoring of "dividend" over "gift."

Ж Ж Ж Ж Ж Ж Ж Ж Ж Ж Ж Ж Ж Ж

There are Catholic grade-school bake sales in Little Italy whose recipes are more complex and demanding than the regulations imposed on Wall St. When the pinstripes of New York baseball teams and the pinstripes of Wall St. business suits converge or criss-cross, two rulebooks are hurled into the fire at once.

Madison Avenue is proof that the illusory is
    quicker than the optic nerve.
Park Avenue is evidence that the parking-structure is
    as priceless as the penthouse.
Wall St. is proof that the credit-crunch is
    quicker than the closing bell.

◻◻◻◻◻◻◻◻◻◻◻◻◻◻◻◻◻◻◻◻◻◻◻◻◻◻◻◻◻◻◻

It is axiomatic up and down Wall St. that if you exclude enough middle your margins will grow obese and if you pinpoint enough portals your parameters will grow porous. Since the wrecking-ball that demolished Ebbets Field was painted like a giant baseball, the wrecking ball that demolishes Wall St. should be painted like a brassy pair of bear testicles.

Some of Wall St.'s several purgatories fall
    in between the perp-walk and the prayer-breakfast,
in between the slip-resistant sidewalk and the scoliosis seminar,
    and in between the gourmet grill-mark
        and the failing-grade freezer-burn.

The 90-degree angle is the hairpin holding Manhattan traffic's flowing tresses in place. Every cabbie knows that Manhattan's curbstones are Cartesian contours overcoming the city's otherwise curvilinear chaos.

Generally speaking, yellow taxis stay in Manhattan
    while green taxis travel into the outer boroughs
just as green bananas can travel further than yellow ones
    without fear of over-ripening
and green-eyed envy can penetrate further
    than yellow-eyed jaundice.

A traffic crossing set on an eternal loop is initially a race between wearing out its pedestrian's shoe leather and wearing out its own red, yellow, and green bulbs and eventually a staring contest between two teams of jaywalkers too tired to move.

A five-foot rise in sea-level
    would put a major crimp on Manhattan's bike-rentals
but a ten-foot rise in sea-level
    would take a major bite
        out of Manhattan's sense of "ground floor.'

As a matter of manual fate and digital democracy-in-action, a taxi-ride flagged down with a fresh manicure executing the Hindu mudra for wholeness is no safer than a taxi flagged down with a moth-eaten mitten in between bourbon-swigs.

Hand-powered manual laborer John Henry was felled and defeated by the steam-driven spike-driver, just as the Manhattan bike messenger was hobbled and scarred by the advent of the email attachment.

The after-shocks of the 1929 stock market crash are still rippling, especially now that Black Fridays come in batches and bear markets hibernate until their own shadows wake them. For reasons of self-division and city-splitting, Manhattan now maintains as many consumer antagonists as consumer advocates and as many public aggressors as public defenders in its service-stable.

Manhattan's fluid dynamics have been known to half-freeze
at a barely-fleeting reference to a fiduciary slowdown
and foam over at the vaguest mention of a financial bubble.

ʃɑƷɑʃɑƷɑʃɑƷɑʃɑƷɑʃɑƷɑʃɑƷɑʃɑƷɑʃɑƷ

Someday a Manhattan money-maven's personalized license plate will be so personal it is a thumbprint or a retinal scan. More and more office towers are built on a zigzag contour to afford more corner offices, but a circular building negates the entire prestige of the corner office along a single democratizing curve.

Among Manhattan's managerial class,
some are born by Caesarean section
and some by Caligulan fiat
and some with a Nero-like disdain
for the prospect of civil collapse.

ɬ«ɬ«ɬ«ɬ«ɬ«ɬ«ɬ«ɬ«ɬ«ɬ«ɬ«ɬ«ɬ«ɬ«ɬ«ɬ«ɬ«ɬ

If restricted airspace above the Bankers Trust building can ever charge an access fee based on petro-dollar derivatives, a restricted airspace above the New York Public Library should be able to charge its entrance fee in late-fines-to-come. A small body of water ironically named Collect Pond was once located near where tax-collecting City Hall now stands, like a ghost-before-the-fact.

Manhattan's self-made anthem "New York, New York" mentions the city's "vagabond shoes" but ignores its "market moccasins," "status sandals," "gutter galoshes," "Libertarian loafers," "off-grid Oxfords," and "crosstown clogs."

If an operating theater's audience ever gives a standing ovation to a spinal tap it will owe a squirming ovation to a liver transplant, a squinting ovation to a cornea replacement and a side-stepping ovation to a heart bypass. If the preferred paramedics at a Manhattan hospital hoist a gurney more like a stevedore than a sanitation worker, the preferred pallbearers at a Manhattan funeral parlor hoist a casket more like a delivery boy than a dockworker.

The percentage of actors who were born
    in a New York City hospital
        and died in a Los Angeles bungalow
            is a slanted, Pacific-prone ratio
                that the Delaware Water Gap
                    does nothing to encourage
                        and the San Andreas Fault
                            does nothing to discourage.

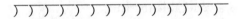

Certain cardiograms accidentally simulate the Manhattan skyline, and certain brain-scans incidentally evoke the tidal currents of the East River, but an X-ray's likeness to a burst of Times Square neon is a dyed-in-the-chromosomes family resemblance.

In a world of prosthetic justice,
    hip replacements for Studio 54 alumni
        would come with a fully rotational
            Latin bassline overdrive gear,
                a drum-break cruise control,
                    and a mirror-ball turn-signal.

If the visiting hours at a Mt. Sinai cancer ward seem longer for a visitor than for a visitee, but the opposite is true at a Mt. Sinai maternity ward, this may mean there are certain kinks in the mortal coil that need mental disentangling.

A revolving door leading into a 5th Avenue emergency room is a reminder of mortality's epic roundabout and fatalism's squeaky spindle. A mail-slot mistakenly placed on said door would require pinpoint accuracy from a mail-carrier-turned-mail-archer.

The greeters at Tiffany's smile more with their clothes than with their lips, the security guards at Tiffany's scowl more with their pistols than with their brows, and the cashiers at Tiffany's applaud more with their receipts than with their palms. Some sales-girls at certain midtown boutiques are expected to become virtuosi of partial customer-ignoring, making Off-the-Rack an in-store version of Some Assembly Required.

"Radio City" is a venerable institution
    and "Video City" is a ratty old retailer
        for reasons that don't require a post-Marxist
            counter-account of the fetish commodity.
                an Ivy League postgraduate marketing degree,
                    or a pair of binoculars
                        able to peer into consumer history
                        to determine.

****
****

If having been a member of a Manhattan hung jury statistically rendered one more indecisive at a Macy's perfume counter, having worked under too many city-planning deadlines might turn one's impulse-shopping into an instinct. At the Saks Fifth Avenue cosmetic counter, pancake makeup that simulates iron-poor anemia should be discouraged before mascara learns how to mimic myopia, rouge learns to imitate a swamp fever, and concealer discovers how to expunge whole identities.

A tag sale becomes a yard sale
 and a garage sale becomes a rummage sale
  as one travels down from the
   laissez-faire economics of Scarsdale
    to the near-barter of the Lower East Side.

Check-out time at the Plaza Hotel is sometimes measured by fountain rather than by clock because check-in at the Ritz-Carlton is sometimes gauged by red carpet rather than reservation and room-service at the Four Seasons is sometimes summoned by stomach-growl rather than by landline.

Most New York bodega owners speak fluent grawlix (@&#!),
 but some transpose their ampersands and their hashtags
  or prematurely utter a forward slash after
   stubbing their tongue on an exclamation point
    during moments of intensely graphic
     customer dispute.

The charity-event applause at a Lincoln Center "recital" tends to feature more wedding-ring-on-pinkie-ring clatter than a cattle-call "concert" at Madison Square Garden does, and considerably less use of sandals as prosthetic clappers than a no-admission "gig" at Coney Island does.

The seating capacity of Carnegie Hall
 and squinting capacity at the Hayden Planetarium
  and spinning capacity of whatever auditorium is
   hosting the Ice Capades
    occasionally try to outsit, outstare,
     and outcircle one another.

A cough in Carnegie Hall is a hundred times more noticed than a yawn at the Yonkers raceway or a worry-scratch at a Whitney opening. Since Grand Central Station has a Hall of Whispers, MoMA should have a Hall of Gasps, the U.N. building a Hall of Mistranslations, and Madison Square Garden a Hall of Collective Groans.

If a Canal St. Hall of Fame ever opens,
   it will feature more tributes to knock-off vendors
      than to pothole repairmen
         and a prayer-flag made from a badly silkscreened tee-shirt
            with its arms slapping in Esperanto semaphore.

ɑʃɑƧɑʃɑƧɑʃɑƧɑʃɑƧɑʃɑƧɑʃɑƧɑʃɑ

A certain percentage of Park Avenue
   is a pay-as-you-go Ponzi pyramid
      whose pointed head was erected
         from the toppled pillars of Tammany Hall.

The squeal caused by the Staten Island Ferry's hull rubbing against the wooden pilings at Whitehall terminal causes shrieking responses from circling herring-gulls, a signature note on New York's avian scale akin to the Sheridan Square lullaby of pigeon-coos and the Tompkins Square signal-alert of a red-tailed hawk's hunger-pangs.

Shuffle the cue-cards for a State of the Borough address and "please be seated" and "next question" and "no comment" all lose their place in "line." There are fine-print amendments to the Manhattan Borough Constitution so fine they should fined for the retinal strain they induce.

The Nobel Prize for nosebleeds
    goes to a Borough of Manhattan city planner
        because the Pulitzer Prize for pulled hamstrings
            goes to a Prospect Park path-maker.

ロロロロロロロロロロロロロロロロロロロロロロロロロ

How local would a single-borough currency need to be before it coagulated into an intransitive token? How often do New York's so-called "vest-pocket" borough parks attract their own lint in the form of loiterers or their own spare change in the form of standers-by?

Sometimes a Manhattan borough president's disapproval ratings
    are figuratively spelled out in sequins
        on the backs of denim jackets in Spanish Harlem
          or in Lower East Side graffiti-bubbles
            swollen to the point of implosion.

✲:✲:✲:✲:✲:✲:✲:✲:✲:✲:✲:✲:✲:✲:✲:✲:

A borough's breeding rate dips in neighborhoods where average income spikes and where each professional acronym (or hereditary abbreviation after a proper name) equals more prophylactic use and every Christmas bonus means one less act of non-immaculate conception.

The burrowing and burrowed-into borough of Manhattan
    commits mass germicide on its handrails,
        occasional termicide on its politicos,
          dismissive dermicide on its skin-cells,
            and rare-but-decisive firmicide on its
            corporations as needed.

Manhattan steers into its skids so scarily its spinouts are its signature. The mica schist that forms a large portion of Manhattan's bedrock can be anagrammed into A Schism Tic for fairly apparent reasons.

Alternate names for Manhattan:
Insomnia National Park,
The Social Darwinism National Open,
Jay-Walker Memorial Lawn,
and the Obscene Gesture Finger Lakes.

✵✵✵✵✵✵✵✵✵✵✵✵✵✵✵✵✵

Manhattan has eclipsed three separate newspapers called the Sun into defunct-ness, perhaps as a pagan tribute to its ongoing affair with all things nocturnal. The op-ed columns of the New York Times, if laid end-to-end, would reach twice to the moon and halfway to the sun before turning into cosmic kindling.

The founding treaties that put New York's business-world into gear put the curse into cursive by double-crossing its "t"'s, spot-checking its "i"'s and crossing its fingers behind its own signatures' backs.

Ж Ж Ж Ж Ж Ж Ж Ж Ж Ж Ж Ж

In Manhattan, someone allergic to avenues is condemned to primarily non-vertical voyages. Most of what is most memorable about Manhattan is also too mobile to mount plaques on, too kinetic to commemorate, and so fleeting it becomes hard to forget because its haste is so high-impact.

In Manhattan's most hidden halls of power
slush funds are not matters of snow-melt
    any more than skunkworks are matters of scent
        or shell companies are shadows cast by crustaceans.

Manhattan keeps in touch with its residual New Amsterdam
by holding annual tulip shows, maintains relations with its inner
Father Knickerbocker by wearing knee-socks, and stays in contact
with its leftover Duke of York by holding high teas in the lobby of
the Carlyle Hotel.

A completely abandoned Manhattan
    would echo more baritone than a vacated Venice
        but more soprano than a depopulated Detroit.

«±«±«±«±«±«±«±«±«±«±«±«±«±«±«±

Manhattan can resemble a failing old console television picture
tube exaggerating the greens in a suitcase full of cash and down-
playing the reds in bullet-wounds. The post-modern pace-setter
transplanted into Manhattan's heart beats at innumerable scandals
per second and mob-scenes per minute, daring cardiac failure and
criminal arrest at once.

When Manhattan wants to promote its own monogram, a
many-sided mortgage on a mansion made of mad-money mints
its own marketplace out of a margin-call. The borough's self-
acclaiming volume cannot be the product of mere uproar but of
downroar and sideroar and slantroar and crossroar as well.

Manhattan is the quantum proof that one can be a nomad, prodigal, vagrant, and marathoner without ever leaving one's home island, neighborhood, block, or building. Manhattan is a specimen of fractal spacetime every time it allows its extra innings to precede its anthems and its overtures to be undermined by its encores.

The crumpled, wadded-up balls of blueprint
    in a city planner's wastebasket
        are the unpairable electrons of the urban atom
            and the unhung ornaments on the evergreen tree
        of New York City's Never-Happened.

CPSIA information can be obtained
at www.ICGtesting.com
Printed in the USA
BVHW030812270922
648045BV00007B/129